Play It from the Heart

What You Learn from Music about Success in Life

J. Steven Moore

Published in partnership with
MENC: The National Association for Music Education

ROWMAN & LITTLEFIELD EDUCATION

A division of
ROWMAN & LITTLEFIELD PUBLISHERS, INC.
Lanham • New York • Toronto • Plymouth, UK

Published in partnership with MENC: The National Association for Music Education

Published by Rowman & Littlefield Education
A division of Rowman & Littlefield Publishers, Inc.
A wholly owned subsidary of
The Rowman & Littlefield Publishing Group, Inc.
4501 Forbes Boulevard, Suite 200, Lanham, Maryland 20706
http://www.rowmaneducation.com

Estover Road, Plymouth PL6 7PY, United Kingdom

British Library Cataloguing in Publication Information Available

Library of Congress Cataloging-in-Publication Data

Moore, J. Steven.
  Play it from the heart : what you learn from music about success in life /
J. Steven Moore.
    p. cm.
  "Published in partnership with MENC: The National Association for Music Education."
  Includes bibliographical references and index.
  ISBN 978-1-61048-369-8 (cloth : alk. paper) — ISBN 978-1-61048-370-4 (pbk. : alk. paper) — ISBN 978-1-61048-371-1
  1. Music and philosophy. 2. Success. 3. Conduct of life. I. MENC, the National Association for Music Education (U.S.) II. Title.

ML3830.M77P5 2011
781.1'7—dc22   2011011022

∞™ The paper used in this publication meets the minimum requirements of American National Standard for Information Sciences—Permanence of Paper for Printed Library Materials, ANSI/NISO Z39.48-1992.

Printed in the United States of America

Contents

Acknowledgments   v

Prelude: I Know This Kid   1

1 Get on the Bandwagon!   5

2 The Creative Process   11

3 Let Excellence Be Your Trademark   21

4 People Are Paramount   31

5 Leadership Lessons   43

6 Individual Responsibility   55

7 Group Interaction in Music   63

8 Developing Group Identity and Loyalty   71

9 Competition and Cooperation within Competition   81

10 Cooperation and Interdependence   91

11 Passion in Performance, Work, and Life   99

12 Putting It Together   109

Postlude: Beyond the Notes   115

Appendix: Reflections from a Band Member   117

Index   119

About the Author   123

Acknowledgments

This book is dedicated to my children, Jameson and Lorian Moore, in hopes that they will have much joy in music and life. As I can never properly thank my own parents, Carolyn Reese and J. Larry Moore, I hope that in some small way this book will express my love and appreciation for all that they have given me. With much love and gratitude I thank my wife, Kimberly Sena Moore, who inspired the original concept and who continues to serve as an inspiration in my life. I would also like to express appreciation to Tom Eblen for his recommendations and considerable editing skills. Heartfelt thanks are also extended to Sheree Hood, Karen Oxley, and Catherine Wilson for their encouragement and support throughout the creative process.

I am most grateful to all my students who gave their heart and soul to music, to their friends, and to me. It's rather common for teachers to learn from their students, and thankfully I have had the privilege of sharing many indelible moments with these remarkable young musicians. I humbly apologize for my shortcomings as a teacher, and I thank them all for their patience, love, and dedication.

Prelude: I Know This Kid

I sat on the couch with tears welling in my eyes. As I read the story of Patrick Henry Hughes, a University of Louisville trumpet player with amazing abilities, I couldn't help but think: *I know this kid*. Not him personally, but I know a lot of kids like him. They love band so much that they will make any sacrifice to be a part of it. I tried not to cry. I felt embarrassed to tear up over a *Sports Illustrated* article, but I was alone, and I can't help the way I feel about people like Patrick Henry Hughes.

Patrick was born without eyes, he can't straighten his legs or arms, and he has several other physical issues some people might characterize as disabilities. And yet he performs with the University of Louisville Marching Band and a couple hundred other kids who love band and sports and playing "My Old Kentucky Home" at the Kentucky Derby. I know this kid. I have had hundreds just like him in my bands at the University of Kentucky, Lafayette High School, and Colorado State University. Well, not *just* like him, but kids who will give you everything they have and come back and ask if you need anything more. Patrick doesn't exactly *march* like the other performers. His father pushes him in his wheelchair through all of the band's intricate movements and formations.

Patrick doesn't focus on his disabilities; he makes the most of his abilities. How do I know? Well, I know this kid. That's why, as I read the article, my chest started shaking and tears streamed down my face. I recalled kids who were marching popsicles in frigid conditions; kids who performed with everything from chicken pox to a mouthful of missing teeth from a car wreck. One kid marched with a transplanted heart—and doctor's orders to not get *too physical*. I remembered the brave rifle girl who gashed her head during a show but kept performing as blood ran down her face and stained her white uniform. (Even I had enough sense to pull her off the field midway through the show. Later that day, after stitches, she marched in the finals competition.)

I KNOW THIS DAD

Although Patrick was born with several disabilities, he has the one ability he needs most—an attitude of possibility. He won't allow himself to be sidelined. He is a star on the field, powered by a desire to perform—and by his father, Patrick John Hughes, who attends every rehearsal and performance with his son. I know this kid, and I know this father. I've admired hundreds of parents like him. I've known parents who sold boxes of citrus, loaded and unloaded trucks full of equipment, and attended dozens of events with their kids. I have seen parents sacrifice for their kids in ways I never understood as a teacher—until I remembered how my own parents did it for me.

Patrick John Hughes, the father, reminds me of the story of Derek Redmond, the track star, who tore his hamstring during an Olympic semifinal heat in 1992. He refused to quit. Even with tears, obvious grief, and intense pain, his determination to continue was apparent with every hobbled step toward the finish line. Sixty-five thousand people cheered in the stands as his father, Jim, pushed through the officials to help his son finish the race. I get emotional over that story, too, every time I encounter it.

Patrick's father has since won several prestigious awards, but no one could have predicted that at the time. He works the night shift at UPS so he can attend classes with his son during the day. After their initial worry and disappointment, Patrick's parents cared for him with the same love and hope as any parents have for their child. I once asked a band parent how all of his kids turned out so well. He replied that he never turned them away when they came to him. I think of that now when my son is climbing on my lap to grab the computer mouse as I work. Patrick's folks first noticed his interest in music when they set him on a piano as an infant. Patrick's attention was noticeable. He began to play the piano at the age of nine months. Now, in addition to playing piano, Patrick sings, composes, and plays trumpet in the University of Louisville Marching Band under the direction of Dr. Gregory Byrne. I know this guy.

I KNOW THIS BAND DIRECTOR

Actually, I really do know him! Greg is a great musician, a smart guy, and one of the nicest people I know. But a genius? What kind of brilliant thought was it to place Patrick on the field with his dad pushing him around in a wheelchair? It was one of those sincere thoughts that come from the heart—the same heart that knows that every person is someone's precious baby. The kind of leadership that says we have a place for everyone in this organization. The kind of vision that sees one more great musician for the band, not a person in a wheelchair. I know this band director and, sometimes, I am this band director. I have had a deaf snare drummer, a legally blind trumpet player, and many students that I swear couldn't carry a tune in a bucket. And they all have played their hearts out in band. But if Patrick had come to me, I would have told him he could perform on the sideline. I would not have conceived of Patrick and his father on the field in formations. I'm sure I would have thought it would be a distraction because I had never seen it done before. Instead of distracting from the band, though, Greg Byrne's vision has *attracted* worldwide attention to the band. Brilliant.

Patrick's father, who had always dreamed of his son starring on the field in athletics, has seen his son achieve national recognition on an athletic field—through music. In addition to *Sports Illustrated*, he has been featured on ABC-TV's *Extreme Makeover: Home Edition* and *The Oprah Winfrey Show*. Patrick has released a CD, cowritten a book, *I Am Potential,* and he is in demand as an inspirational speaker. Visit his website, www.patrickhenryhughes.com, for more about this amazing family that has refused to be limited by disabilities. I know this kid and his family, I love them, and I love band. It has been a good cry.

Chapter One

Get on the Bandwagon!

You don't have to have been in a band, or love band, to understand the principles in this book. You just have to love people, desire excellence, and want to achieve success in the organizations in your life. Achieving human potential, celebrating the achievements of others, and following your bliss are universal. Music provides a unique path to discovery, and I hope you will find the stories and people in this book uplifting. These principles can apply to people of every walk of life. No matter which drummer we march to, we all follow a similar path of shared emotion. I know I will not be able to do justice to the wisdom that has been bestowed on me by my teachers, the love given to me by my family, or the hearts shared with me by my students. But I believe I owe it to these people to play this one from the heart.

Everybody loves a parade. Everybody loves a band. People want to "strike up the band!" and "get on the bandwagon!" The expression "to beat the band" is to make enough noise to drown it out—to exceed everything. Why do bands inspire such love and passion? What makes a band such a special organization? (For the record: orchestras, choirs, theatre, and dance troupes are also special. But for clarity, ease of reading, and my familiarity with the subject, I am going to stick with bands. Just know I love string players, singers, actors, and dancers, too.) Exactly what is it about a band that engenders such a high level of commitment on the part of its members? Why do bands continue to exist in an age of on-demand digital music downloads?

For one thing, people feel a need to belong to something bigger than themselves. No doubt, this can be achieved in various kinds of organizations. Two that come to mind are sports teams and corporations. Bands

5

share many characteristics with sports teams, but there are some important differences. Sports teams compete with fewer people at any given time: five in basketball, nine in soccer, eleven in football. By comparison, bands usually have anywhere from fourteen to two hundred members. Some of the largest marching bands exceed four hundred members—all performing at once! In band, no one rides the bench. Everyone is a starter and plays the entire performance. Each person is vital. Bands don't pull a person out for missing a note and send in a substitute with fresh chops. Bands also share certain attributes with corporations. But businesses are driven by the bottom line. Rarely is profit the most important consideration in a band.

This is not a sports book or a business book. The purpose of a sports team is to win. The purpose of a business is to make a profit. The purpose of a band is to make music and uplift the human spirit. However, there are principles that have been influenced by sports and corporate paradigms. In reverse, these principles will apply to sports teams and business organizations. This performing arts paradigm provides a path to success, a blueprint for achieving levels of excellence, and principles that apply to any area of life that involves group cooperation and shared goals.

A unique quality of band is that it mimics society in its inclusiveness and diversity. It is for everyone; not just the tall ones, the quick ones, the smart ones, the strong ones, or the pretty ones. Band emphasizes group achievement. It is not like playing golf, tennis, or solo trumpet. There's nothing wrong with individual achievement in sports or the arts. But band—like this book—is about the individual in a group setting. It is about dreaming a goal with your friends and colleagues, giving yourself over to the needs of the group, and experiencing the thrill of achieving much more than any individual can accomplish alone. It is about the group dynamic in action, how to excel in a group, and how to create a harmonious, cooperative spirit in your organization. You can't do it all by yourself, you need each other. There is no greater lesson than to learn to be responsible to the group, to voluntarily give up your individual needs for the good of the group, and to share in the exhilaration of group accomplishment. It is invigorating to be part of something that is bigger than yourself and to know that it couldn't have been done without you.

We all need other people in life, from birth to our passing. All of us, even those who work independently, must function with others to be successful. This skill is noted on our earliest report cards: "Johnny plays well with others!" Some people are leaders in organizations; others are followers. But, at some point, *everyone* leads, regardless of his or her job or title. This book examines bands as an example of perhaps the most cooperative organizations in society. In fact, the definition of a band is a group of people who are united in a common purpose. These musical groups can help us learn how to synchronize with others to achieve joy, harmony, and productivity within any organization.

We all love music, and most of us have felt the effect of its vibrations. We have been moved to dance, cheer, and cry by the power of music. With music as the product, it is no wonder that band leaders and members have developed processes for working together in literal harmony. This book explores strategies for finding meaning and happiness in your life, for achieving success in your participation in groups, and for creating high-performing and harmonious organizations by using the principles of the most finely tuned, rhythmically precise, socially cooperative, and passionately loved organizations in the world—our nation's finest bands.

HOW TO READ THIS BOOK

It was just another message from a former student on a social networking website. "How are you? What are you doing these days?" I love hearing from my former students and learning about their postband lives. But the comments from Heather Erbe, a flautist with an effervescent personality, really struck a chord.

> producing amazing music and getting the best out of every musician . . . incredible four-year lesson on excellence . . . shaped my thinking and molded me to give my best in everything I do . . . set the bar very high and we rose to it . . . people rise to the level of others' expectation . . . always setting the standard high . . . we work together in Mary Kay as Directors . . . we've talked a lot about the standard of excellence we were molded into in band, and we are both reaping rewards from that now.

Heather and her high school friend, Kendra Rumford, have risen to the top 2 percent of salespeople in the multibillion-dollar Mary Kay cosmetics company. I read this poignant letter to my wife, Kimberly, a musician and former drum major. She replied, "Why don't you write that book? You know, the one about the principles people learn from being in band." Because I always listen to my wife, this book is about the experience of being in band and how it can lead to success in many aspects of life.

First, you must understand why I am so entrenched in the band paradigm. My father, J. Larry Moore, was a band director. He grew up playing piano, accordion, and baritone. He became a nationally renowned director of high school bands and an inspiration to thousands of young people, including me. My mother, Carolyn Reese, played flute and taught majorettes and color guard members. I have a wonderful photograph of her in a 1950s band uniform. Her band director was George "Pop" Weekes. In rehearsal, "Pop" taught music and his wife, Sarah "Mom" Weekes, enforced discipline. I played trumpet in my father's band, as did my older foster sister, Judy Flack. My younger sister, Jina Herndon, played clarinet and was an incredible performer in the color guard. My wife sings and plays flute, piano, and several other instruments. She now helps people as a scientifically based music therapist. So, I and everyone in my family, and nearly everyone I have ever loved, is a musician who has been in band.

But I don't think you have to have been in band to learn and use the principles in this book. I have never played organized football or basketball, yet I have used many of the principles from great coaches in my life and career. Similarly, I have never worked for a large corporation, but I have learned a great deal from the best business leaders. As society moves toward more cooperative organizations, there is much we can learn from bands and other musical groups. How do I know? The vast majority of people who participate in band do not go on to become professional performers, music teachers, or therapists. Instead, they hold every leadership position in society, from mother to president of the United States. And most of them have been inspired by their band experience. It is common to think of a band as a group of instrumentalists playing music of a particular style: marching band, concert band, rock band, or mariachi band. But the word has a broader definition: A band is a group of people united by a common purpose. You can think of a band as any group of people functioning together. A troop. A tribe. A band of outlaws. A band of protesters. A band of brothers. A band also binds things together. A wedding band symbolizes the unity of two people in marriage. The root word comes from old French, *bande*, as in *banner*, a group of soldiers identified

As I graduate with a master's degree in civil engineering, I realize that perhaps all the most important things I needed to know for a future in engineering came not from my engineering classes, but from my experience in the department of music. I've learned to listen carefully to those around me, for if you do not play together in harmony, the outcome will not be understood. I've learned that creative expression is often the most effective means of communication. I've learned the responsibility in working with a group, for the quality of the group is dependent upon the quality of the individual. I've learned that consistency and hard work by a leader can foster consistency and hard work by those he or she leads. I've learned the value of working and planning ahead—it is not possible for the human system to learn a symphony by cramming in one night. I've learned that you must be emotionally connected to what you are playing . . . or what you are drawing, designing, building, or planning—because that connection will result in a melody or plan or system or structure that will make a difference in someone's life—an effect that makes being a musician or an engineer extremely rewarding.

In the Colorado State University wind ensemble you are not a number or another body in a chair—you are someone your director knows, someone your section knows, because there is that emotional connection—the one that is required to affect others—that connects you not only to what you are doing but also to the others who are doing it with you.

—Linda Riley, program coordinator,
Oregon Renewable Energy Center,
Oregon Institute of Technology

by its standard (a flag on a pole raised as a rallying point). Most appropriately, it also is a phonetic variant of *bond*. To apply these stories and examples from the musical world of bands to your life, feel free to substitute the words *organization* or *group* each time you see the word *band*. These ideas apply to almost any group of people united for a common purpose. So, let's jump on the bandwagon!

Chapter Two

The Creative Process

THE CBAS OF SUCCESS:
CONCEIVE IT, BELIEVE IT, ACHIEVE IT

Most people agree that the purpose of life is to be happy. One of the great joys in life is purposefully conceiving, creating, and enjoying your dreams. This is creativity in the sense of causing something to happen that comes from your thoughts or imagination. I once heard a show on National Public Radio in which a musician was asked to comment on his success. His answer resonated with me as much as his music, as it describes the creative process perfectly: "Conceive It, Believe It, Achieve It."

CONCEIVE IT

Note Card on the Mirror

One afternoon, I dropped by the home of Thurmas and Madge Reynolds to deliver my director's column for the band newsletter. Thurmas and Madge were terrific band parents, and Madge had taken on the job of newsletter editor. Their daughter, Heather, played clarinet in my band at Lafayette High School in Lexington, Kentucky. Thurmas was a dedicated member of the band parents' association. In his spare time, he earned a living as the school's principal—and my boss. Thurmas, a former coach, had a knack for entertaining and uplifting Lafayette's students, staff, and faculty. I thought of him as principal and chief motivator. The Reynolds lived in an upscale home in one of my favorite Lexington neighborhoods, so upon arriving I asked for a tour. After admiring the *two* staircases, I walked into Heather's room. I was immediately impressed because I had rarely seen a teenager's room so neat! I saw that Heather had a note card taped to her dresser mirror. On it she had written:

1. Straight A's
2. All-State Band
3. Drum Major

Clearly, Heather had dared to dream of herself as a good student, a great musician, and a leader of the most popular organization in the school, the marching band. The conception began as a thought, was formulated into words, and was crystallized into goals. Most appropriately, she had placed them on the mirror as if to say, "If it is to be, it is up to me." The next school year, Heather had a 4.0 grade point average and played in the first clarinet section of the Kentucky All-State Band, which was no small achievement. And, as the band marched down Broadway in New York City for the Macy's Thanksgiving Day Parade, the only person who could upstage Santa Claus was our dynamic drum major in her glittering costume: Heather Reynolds.

Letter on the Locker

Heather's goal setting reminds me of a story I once read in *Reader's Digest*. I can't vouch for every detail or even its authenticity, but the message rings true. A high school student placed the letter *V* on his locker at a time in life when most of his classmates were more concerned about letters on their jackets. He was vague when his friends asked him about it, but he said that each day when he opened his locker he was reminded of his goal. The meaning of the *V* eventually became clear to his friends when he delivered the commencement speech as the school's valedictorian.

M for Midwest

Influenced by this story, I placed an *M* above my desk. The *M* served as a reminder of my goal for the band to perform at the annual Midwest

International Band and Orchestra Clinic in Chicago. Each day, I considered if my actions were moving me closer to my goal or further away. This was a long-term dream, and I knew it could not be rushed. But I also knew that if I built a program that was even close to being considered to perform at this prestigious convention of music educators, many students would benefit and I would be proud of the accomplishment. I received many rejection letters along the way, but eventually we were invited. We performed in 1993, and it will remain one of the highlights of my life.

There must be some magic left in that office: The orchestra director who works there now, Jennifer Grice, called recently to ask me to conduct her group in a performance at the Midwest International Band and Orchestra Clinic. I can't take any credit for this incredible accomplishment, but it still warms my heart.

I Think, Therefore I Create

All of these achievements begin with a thought. What do you want? In your heart of hearts, what do you really want? Sometimes the question is better phrased what do *we* want, as we are often cocreating with others. Start with the ideal. In a perfect world, how would this work? If you could have anything you want, what would it be? If you could be anything you want, what would it be? Many people begin with an image in their mind. When you consciously imagine your goal, it is called creative visualization. I was first introduced to this idea by the book *Psycho-Cybernetics: A New Way to Get More Living Out of Life* by Maxwell Maltz. I learned that Jerry Claiborne, the five-time national football coach of the year, asked each player on his University of Kentucky team to read this book. Later, I found a less scientific approach to the same process, described in *Creative Visualization: Use the Power of Your Imagination to Create What You Want in Your Life* by Shakti Gawain.

The Rehearsal in Your Mind

Of course, you are not limited to just visual imagery. You can bring any of your senses and emotions to this creative process. Musicians often use this "rehearsal in the mind" as they prepare for a performance. This describes a theoretical "mind rehearsal" for a solo recital, with the entire scene going perfectly:

> Taste a drink of refreshing water and take a deep, relaxing breath. Stride confidently across the stage, turn toward the receptive audience, and respond with a warm smile. Smell the flower arrangement next to the piano and nod to the pianist. Feel the experience of playing every note with clarity of technique and beauty of expression. Hear the warm tone and pure intonation of each note. Focus on the music throughout the performance. Look into the audience and enjoy the sincere and enthusiastic applause.

When a musician "rehearses" the performance in this way, the mind doesn't know the difference between the visualization and the performance. As the actual performance occurs, the musician "remembers" the visualized performance as though she has done it many times. The musician draws upon past creative visualizations to increase her ability to perform in the "now moment."

As you visualize, imagine everything going perfectly. Instead of thinking about everything that could go wrong, imagine everything going exactly as it should. Use your mind to create the image, sound, smell, taste, and feel of your desire. Dream big. To achieve your goal, attract the help of others with your strong vision. While most people think in images, we also are capable of thinking in words, numbers, and music. Most musicians are able to audiate—to hear the music in their mind. The ability to think in music is one of the hallmarks of a musically literate person. Therefore, imagination is more than the ability to create images in your mind. Visualize, audiate, think in words, and think in music to create your concept. This is most successful when you are inspired but relaxed. A feeling of relaxed concentration will allow you to keep your focus on the thought. Often, inspiration comes quickly and from an outside source. Some of the best thoughts about goals at work may be inspired by influences outside your profession: musicals, visual art, literature, science, film, sports, politics, religion, or simple kindness between people. Feel free to choose that which you want to bring into your life and ignore that which you don't.

BELIEVE IT

Approach this new door with great confidence in your heart, for you have prepared well for this moment. Open each new door with trust, holding your hopes and dreams very near . . . knowing that the world is waiting for the excellence and the love you carry with you.

—M. E. Miro

You have a deliberate thought. You have considered the thought enough to know that it is your sincere desire, at least at this time. You have turned this thought over in your mind, and now you are ready to consider it in your heart. If your thought is to become reality, then it will require your full commitment to its validity and the faith that you can achieve it. It is not enough to see it, hear it, smell it, or taste it—you must *feel* it. When you have belief, you infuse the idea with the energy it will need to thrive. In music, you can play a bunch of notes or you can play with feeling, expression, and soul. Without conviction, music is merely a technical exercise. In order to communicate with—to *move*—your audience, you must infuse the music with your heart. If you don't feel it, the audience won't feel it. You can't give away what you don't possess.

Conductors are encouraged to play only music that they are *passionate* about. Performers are urged to get their instrument out of its case only when they feel *passionate* about making music. If you emotionally connect with a thought, you are harmonizing with the idea. In music, to play in harmony you must become aware of, and in tune with, the surrounding vibrations. This is similar to tuning into what you want. When you believe in your idea, you have confidence in it, even though there may be no evidence you are correct in believing it. Many people are fond of saying, "I'll believe it when I see it!" In order to bring a new idea into your life, *you must believe it before you see it*. If you are in an organization, the group will need to believe it before it is achieved. One of the truly exhilarating experiences in life is to achieve a group goal that may have seemed unlikely or impossible. It is often said that if you think you can or if you think you can't, you're right. But if, in your heart, you can transform your doubt into a belief—transform an idea from the impossible to the possible—then the idea has a chance to develop and flourish.

Praying from the Heart

One of the best examples of true belief in my life came at an early age, and it had little to do with music. My parents divorced when I was five. My father went to graduate school in Nashville, and my mother moved to Louisville to teach elementary school. I lived with my mother and visited my father occasionally. I loved both of my parents, and I wanted very much for us all to be together again as a family. I remember my grandmother telling me to pray every night and that if I did, it would be possible. I believed her. Each night, I got on my knees, clasped my hands, and prayed as hard as I could for my parents to get back together. I prayed with the complete faith, belief, and conviction of a five-year-old. In retrospect, it was risky for Grandmom to encourage me in this way, but by the end of the year, my dad had accepted a band-directing job in Ashland, Kentucky, and my mom and I were on our way to live with him. I remember feeling happy about this development—and also by the promise that there was a huge toy store in town. The divorce was annulled, a legal term for saying it never happened, and my parents stayed together for another fourteen years, until I went to college. There is no doubt they loved each other; my little sister, Jina, was born in Ashland a few years after they got back together. But I also know that Dad told me he couldn't stand to be away from Mom and me, and I have to believe that the outcome was affected because I believed.

I've come to recognize in myself and in others that what we *believe* is possible determines what *is* possible. Since most of us are rational, our beliefs are also rational. This keeps it real, as I don't honestly believe that I will ever be a professional basketball player or swim the English Channel. However, the game is over before it is begun unless you allow yourself the possibility of believing in your possibilities.

Act as If You Already Are

The great inventor Charles F. Kettering said, "Believe and act as if it were impossible to fail." I took my band for several years to the Contest of Champions at Middle Tennessee State University in Murfreesboro, Tennessee. While we performed well, we never won the Grand Championship. Standing in the shadow of my father, who had won that contest more than anyone else, I was beginning to wonder if I had the ability to lead my band to the highest level. One day, my friend and colleague Allen Goodwin said to me, "When you win the Contest of Champions . . ." He said it with such sincerity and conviction that I was surprised, but somehow soothed. With a PhD from North Texas State University (now the University of North Texas) and a room full of inventions, Allen was one of the most intelligent people I knew. Because he believed in me, I began to believe as well, and I started to act as though it would happen. I released the anxiety about when we might win, and I relaxed and began to enjoy the process of creating a championship band. In a couple of years, his belief in me proved justified. We won the contest five straight years—one more time than my father had.

Owning Your Limitations

Until then, I was good at listing all of the reasons why I had not, and probably could not, win with the band I had at Lafayette. Of course, none of them were my fault. Master leadership mentor Tim Lautzenheiser once said, "If you argue for your limitations, you get to own them." Instead of constantly thinking of all the reasons you cannot achieve a goal, act as though you have already achieved it. This puts you in a mindset that you or your group is capable of accomplishing the goal. Most goals that are worthy of your dreams will require your consistent attention and likely will involve taking risks. In Kentucky, we are fond of saying, "You can't jump a creek in two jumps." At some point, there will need to be a leap of faith. If you notice hesitation or negativity, don't beat yourself up over it, because that gives too much energy to negative thoughts. In meditation, when you are trying to clear your mind of all thoughts, you are advised to notice a thought like a leaf flowing down a stream. It's there, it moves on, and the stream continues to flow. Allow your stream to flow with positive thoughts and don't allow resistance. There is a great book title, *You Can't Afford the Luxury of a Negative Thought,* by Peter McWilliams. It is such a great title that I haven't read the book. Of course, there will always be naysayers. Notice them, and let them flow on by. If you have an idea and you can see the path to achieving it, then it is possible. I can't tell you how I know that to be true, but I can tell you that it has happened so many times in my life that I believe it!

ACHIEVE IT

The price of success is hard work, dedication to the job at hand, and the determination that whether we win or lose, we have applied the best of ourselves to the task at hand.

—Vince Lombardi

I grew up idolizing the legendary football coach Vince Lombardi. My father quoted him often. I revered the Green Bay Packers, and I read Jerry Kramer's team diary, *Instant Replay*. An interesting fact about Lombardi is that he didn't become a head coach until he was forty-five years old. One of Lombardi's great players was Bill Curry, who once coached at the University of Kentucky. He was the first person I heard say, "Many people have the will to win, but few people have the will to prepare." It's natural that we look to sports figures for inspiration to achieve goals. In sports competition, the goals are clear and the results concrete. Kentucky basketball icon Adolph Rupp, one of the most-winning coaches of all time, was famous for saying, "If it doesn't matter whether you win or lose, why do they keep score?" But often, realizing our goals and dreams is not about competition. I once had a sign painted on our band's practice area that said, "It is easier to be better than someone else than it is to be your best." But once you conceive it and believe it, how do you achieve it?

Guarantee Your Success

Action gives power to thoughts and words. Although they are elementary, I like the sayings, "Plan your work and work your plan," and "If you fail to plan, you plan to fail." Determine what will be necessary to move from point A to point B in your quest. For an idea to be successful, you need to envision the process by which your success can happen. After you have decided on the path to achieving your goal, it will be necessary to follow through. In other words: prepare, commit, and execute.

Conceive It, Believe It, Achieve It
also may be expressed as
Aspiration, Inspiration, Perspiration!

Chicks Send Me High!

While it may be true that nothing worth achieving comes easily, it is possible that your desires may come to you with great joy. The achievement of the goal will require striving, but it may not necessarily be full of effort. Much of life's fun happens in the creative process. University of Chicago psychology professor Mihaly Csikszentmihalyi calls this "optimal experience flow." (Terrific professor; tough name. Perhaps this fun, phonetic pronunciation will help: *Me-high! Chicks-send-me-high!*)

Dr. Csikszentmihalyi suggests that an optimal experience in life can be achieved by creating flow in your activities. Flow is a condition whereby you become completely and joyfully immersed in an activity. You often lose track of time and don't experience anxiety or boredom. The best moments in life often occur when you are trying to accomplish something worthwhile, usually something that is challenging yet attainable. He describes flow as having nine elements, which I have taken the liberty of paraphrasing and applying to a music rehearsal:

1. You have clear goals every step of the way.
You play the notes correctly.
2. You get immediate feedback.
You hear the wrong notes.
3. Your skill level meets the challenge.
The music is hard, but not too hard.
4. You think about what you are doing.
You focus on each note in turn.
5. You are not distracted.
You ignore everything except the music.
6. You are not worried about failing.
If you miss a note, it isn't a crisis.
7. You aren't self-conscious.
You play as if no one else is listening.
8. You lose track of time.
Rehearsal is over before you know it.
9. You enjoy the activity just to do it—it is "autotelic."
You play music simply for the fun of it.

Kiss and Autotelic

Some activities, by their very nature, are autotelic—they are enjoyable to do for no other reason than doing them. (*Auto*, meaning "self," as in *autograph*, and *–telic*, meaning "purpose.") Activities such as drawing, painting, sculpting, dancing, sailing, swimming, running, discovering, and even kissing can be described as autotelic. While there certainly may be an extrinsic purpose to them, people often engage in these activities for the sheer joy of it. In fact, an extrinsic purpose can spoil the enjoyment. Notice that all are "being" or "doing" activities. "Having," while certainly worthwhile, may involve activities with more effort—unless you create a path to acquiring material things that is enjoyable for you.

Do what you love and you will never work a day in your life

The best of all possible worlds is to achieve your goals and desires by engaging in the optimal experience of flow. When you set out to accomplish a goal, create your plan in such a way that you can experience joy in the process, not just the result. You have heard the saying, "Life is a journey, not a destination. Enjoy the trip." This is even more important as you realize that after you achieve one goal, there will always be another and another and another. Perhaps this will influence the original creation of your desire. When you "conceive it," you must also conceive the process that will be necessary to "achieve it." My career goal is to have a great musical ensemble in which all of the performers are engaged in joyous music making and music learning. In order to achieve this goal, each day I rehearse and perform inspired music with wonderful people. Any time I begin to get frustrated, I return to the core principle of making beautiful music with people I love. If you can find a joyous process to achieve the desired product, then you will enjoy the journey as well as the destination.

Chapter Three

Let Excellence Be Your Trademark

He has called on the best that was in us . . . We might not be the best, and none of us were, but we were to make the effort to be the best. "After you have done the best you can," he used to say, "the hell with it."

— Senator Robert F. Kennedy, tribute to his father,
Joseph P. Kennedy. Read at Joseph Kennedy's funeral by
Senator Edward Kennedy, November 20, 1969

How many times have I heard, "If it's worth doing, it's worth doing right!" That could be my family's motto. My paternal grandfather passed away before I was born, but I was told that his farm was the cleanest, most well-kept farm in central Kentucky. Perhaps that is why I want the Colorado State University Center for the Arts building to be clean and orderly whenever we have visitors. I saw a newspaper clipping in which my grandfather was named the outstanding sheep farmer at the Kentucky State Fair. There must have been nary a breeze the day the apple fell from the tree, as many years later his son (my father) also won the state fair, not as a sheep farmer but as a shepherd of students (a band director). I don't want to say my dad is competitive; let's just say he likes to count. I've seen him count and compare the number of students who made the all-state band, the number of "superior" ratings received at the solo and ensemble festival, and even the number of bands we competed against during the course of a season. It wasn't about narcissism but about seeing where we stood in comparison to others. If we were behind others, he spent every spare minute figuring out how to improve the situation. Now, I don't want to say he is overly competitive, but he will play you for blood in a game of horseshoes. So, I grew up with high expectations.

In my junior year of high school, I was grounded from driving for three months for each B on my report card. I got three Bs, for a total of nine months—tantamount to a death sentence for a teenage boy. Thanks to a family friend, though, I got a reprieve after a few months. My mom wasn't much different. She won several state championships with her majorette squads and rarely lost a color guard trophy once that activity became popular in the 1970s. I'm sure most families have a similar legacy they embrace as a source of pride.

But excellence isn't just about competition. While sometimes competing is unavoidable, I have come to believe that cooperation is more important than competition and that there is enough of the good stuff to go around for everyone. Competition has its place: It is valuable for clarifying goals and motivating people to embrace excellence. However, it isn't necessary for achieving excellence. Intrinsic desire, regardless of outside recognition, is deeper, more lasting, and in the long run, more satisfying.

Quality is vital in organizations. To attract the best people to your group, it must be first class; it must be an organization that people are proud to associate with. Ray Cramer, the director of bands emeritus at Indiana University, is known to say, "Don't let good get in the way of great!" In a music ensemble, quality is important for many reasons: You owe it to the audience, you owe it to the other members of the ensemble, and you owe it to the composer who is counting on you, the performer, to artistically deliver her creation to the world. Furthermore, in music, 99 percent just isn't good enough. Ask an ensemble of sixty people to play a phrase of music while deliberately playing only one wrong note. The result is a hilarious musical disaster. It never fails to prove that every sound—as well as every person—is vital to success.

If you truly excel, you honor the process as well as the product. The end never justifies the means if you are looking for long-term sustainability for yourself and your group. In honoring process, you also honor people. You are open to their ideas and, by extension, you are open to creativity and innovation. Expect excellence, and you will get what you expect. When you are knee-deep in the "CBA's of Success," how do you know that you are creating with merit and virtue? Is it possible to avoid humorist Garrison Keillor's good-natured trap of self-deception, where "all the women are strong, all the men are good-looking, and all the children are above average"?

PRACTICE THE WAY YOU PERFORM

One of the ways to achieve excellence in a musical ensemble is to "practice the way you perform, and perform the way you practice." If every performer approaches every minute of rehearsal like it is the most important performance of the season, the result is nothing short of spectacular. Our championship Lafayette Band often rehearsed as though it was the final performance for the state championship in front of twenty thousand fans. When that championship performance finally arrived, band members didn't have to "find an extra gear" or "turn it on"; they just went about their normal routine of being incredible. There were no adrenalin-induced mistakes, no overplaying; just the relaxed concentration and passion the band practiced in every rehearsal. The fabulous by-product of this approach is that every rehearsal becomes a thrilling, artistic experience.

THE TEMPLATE OF EXCELLENCE

After a concert, a fan rushed up to the famous violinist Fritz Kreisler and gushed, "I'd give my whole life to play as beautifully as you do." Kreisler replied, "I did."

—"Bits & Pieces," *Economics Press*, Vol. R, No. 2

Your experiences influence your expectations. My mentor, University of South Carolina Director of Bands James Copenhaver, and I once discussed why a particular band was not as good as expected. The band director was an excellent musician, a solid teacher, and a sincere person. People genuinely liked him and enjoyed being around him. But everyone agreed that the product was not very good. Why? Mr. Copenhaver explained that the director had never experienced true excellence. Therefore, he did not expect or ask for excellence from his own band. People's vision often is limited by what they have seen in the past. My goals as a high school band director included playing at the Midwest International Band and Orchestra Clinic and winning the Contest of Champions. Both were worthy goals; many terrific directors have never walked on stage at Midwest or climbed the stairs of the awards platform at the Contest of Champions. However, these were goals I had participated in; therefore, my vision was limited to these goals. As I reflect, my only regret is that I didn't dream bigger. So, we all must ask ourselves, what is shaping our expectations of excellence?

FOCUSING ON WHY YOU WANT IT,
NOT JUST WHAT YOU WANT

One of my most valued possessions is an old black-and-white photo of my father's band playing at the 1970 Midwest International Band and Orchestra Clinic. I know many of the students in the picture, and it includes my piano teacher, Patricia Patrick. The conductor's music stand is slightly askew. My father's band at Paul Blazer High School in Ashland, Kentucky, was the first concert band from Kentucky to perform at Midwest. While I was too young to be in the band, I attended the concert in the ornate ballroom of the now-demolished Sherman House in Chicago. I was overwhelmed with the quality and emotion of the performance. I point to that concert as the seminal event in my decision to become a band director.

As a director, one of my goals was to perform at Midwest and put my father back on the stage as a conductor. I applied several times and received polite rejection letters: "Thank you for your application . . . due to the large number of terrific ensembles that applied . . . we regret to inform you . . ." I almost had them memorized. At some point, I let go of that dream and did some serious soul-searching about what it was I really wanted. I came to the realization that what I most desired was a band that was *capable* of playing at Midwest. I wanted a program that had incredible individual musicians, a strong concert band, marching band, jazz ensembles, and chamber music. I wanted a program that was balanced in woodwinds, brass, percussion, and color guard; a program that was brimming with energy and full of people enjoying the process of making music. I set about creating that program, and I paid less attention to the extrinsic goal of performing at Midwest. Within a few years, the program I wanted was coming to pass. Soon, I got another letter from the organizers of the Midwest Clinic: "Thank you for your application . . . congratulations . . . we would like to invite you . . .!"

I now keep my color picture of the 1993 Lafayette Band performing at Midwest hanging next to my father's old picture. I remember all of the students. My father is standing next to me with a baton in his hand, and the conductor's music stand is perfectly straight.

COMPARING YOUR CURRENT SITUATION TO THE IDEAL

The Contest of Champions, which began in 1962, is the nation's oldest marching band competition. From 1975 to 1979, my father, J. Larry Moore, directed the Lafayette Band to championships in four out of five years. I was a member of that band for two years, 1975 and 1976, and served on his staff for three years, from 1977 to 1979. Because of that experience, I knew what it took to win. In my mind, I knew what the winning band sounded like, looked like, and felt like. When I became Lafayette's director, I set about making sure our band matched those expectations. When I heard the band, I compared it to the template in my mind. As I watched the way the band members moved, I compared it to the template in my mind. When it didn't match, I looked for every way possible to move it toward the ideal. After several years, the band's performance matched the ideal in my mind.

Today, my template of excellence is more likely to involve the world's greatest bands and orchestras. Through recordings, conventions, and other live performances, I have experienced some of the finest bands in the world. When I listen to my own ensemble, I compare its sound to the template in my mind that was formed by listening to the finest musical ensembles in the world. The template has also been shaped by my own ideal sound for the composition we are playing. When it doesn't match, I use every tool at my disposal to create a sound that matches or improves upon the template.

When you evaluate your level of excellence, it is important to honestly examine your template. What experiences are shaping your template? Are they the best possible? Do they reflect excellence? Is this template appropriate for the situation, or should you create a new one? Be honest with yourself. Always seek improvement through professional development and

exposure to the world's best in your field. This is how you can know that
your template of excellence is valid and continually improving.

REVELLI = EXCELLENCE

There is a saying among educators, "Teachers teach how they were taught,
not how they were taught to teach." While it is natural to be heavily influenced by your own experiences, it is important not to fall into the trap of
mediocrity. Take every opportunity to enrich your direct experience with
the very best in your field. Visit the most successful programs, study with
the most-qualified teachers, and seek the most inspiring mentors. Enlarge
your circle of experience. William Revelli (1902–1994) was one of the
most renowned band directors of all time. His bands at Hobart, Indiana,
won the national concert band festival, and his bands at the University
of Michigan were legendary for their excellence. Revelli's influence still
permeates all areas of my profession. He had a template of excellence that
far exceeded most mortals. When you came close to achieving that level,
it was heavenly; when you fell short, heaven help you. How did he create
this template? He attended rehearsals and concerts of one of the world's
greatest ensembles, the Chicago Symphony Orchestra. He studied privately on all of the instruments with players in the symphony, who were
some of the finest musicians in the world. Revelli knew excellence, and
he was not afraid to ask his ensembles for it. If you played with Revelli,
you experienced excellence and were forever changed.

EXCELLENCE IN PROCESS AND PRODUCT

When developing a template of excellence, most people envision the
product. It is essential to imagine the product the way it should be. However, it also is important to imagine the process. Most products are the
result of a system. For example, at band camp we don't teach a show, we
teach a system of learning the show and perfecting the performance. If
band members master the system of learning at camp, they will perform
the show with excellence and have a successful season.

The process by which a product is created is vital. The manner in which people are treated and included while developing a product affects the product as well as the longevity of an organization. If people are treated well, future product quality is enhanced. Involving people in the creation of a product is vital because it allows each person to have an emotional investment in the system and the outcome. Motivation by fear (extrinsic motivation) is fast and effective in the short term. But intrinsic motivation produces deeper, more lasting investment and attachment to the organization. Dictatorships can be clean and effective in the short term, but representative democracies, while slower and messier, respect process and are more successful in the long term. If a person is handed a task without understanding it or being involved in its creation, he may do it, but perhaps without joy. No one is interested in being a puppet, so it is important to invest in a process that involves people. Not only is it ethically correct, it is more effective. Phil Jackson, the legendary coach of the Chicago Bulls and Los Angeles Lakers, describes his philosophy of winning this way: "Give everybody, from the stars to the No. 12 player on the bench, a vital role on the team . . . build a team that would blend individual talent with a heightened group consciousness." He now has a National Basketball Association championship ring for each finger and thumb on both hands.

POWER VS. FORCE

Recently, a colleague asked me metaphorically, "What do you do when the people around you are playing out of tune?" This is an important consideration, as there are times when the reality of the situation does not match your template of excellence. Sometimes, it is so far off that it will take more than a nudge to correct. There is no doubt that a strong leader can move reality closer to the desired outcome. Sometimes, the inclination is to bully it into compliance. I have been known to show passion, get excited, raise my voice, and *demand* excellence. (I prefer to think of it as "believing" in the potential of band members for the good of all involved.) But the more desirable approach is to attract excellence to you like a magnet. If you embody that which you want, then people who feel the same way and who share a common purpose will be attracted to you.

This approach feels better and, in the long run, is more sustainable than forcing a square peg into a round template of excellence.

For many years, I tracked the attendance of Lafayette Band members, often posting it in the band room. I told them that their attendance rate would equal their score at the state marching band championship. How's that for extrinsic motivation? The funny thing is that it often did; the band members' attendance rate was usually around 97 percent, and we generally scored near that number. As a side note, it amused me that the school's faculty attendance rate was usually about 93 percent. Some years, I took a hard line regarding attendance, with strict penalties for missing rehearsal—public admonishment and obvious negative body language when anyone asked for permission to miss. Other years, I managed to take a more relaxed approach and respond with something similar to "I'm sure you have considered every possibility and you wouldn't miss this important rehearsal unless there was no other choice. Thanks for caring, and I wish you well at your event." While both approaches rendered approximately the same attendance rate, I can tell you which one feels better and, in the long run, produces a more joyful experience for the band member.

This approach is best expressed in a book Tim Lautzenheiser shared with me, *Power vs. Force*, by David Hawkins. The entire book is thought provoking, but there are two pages (146 and 147) that stand out. Dr. Hawkins provides a list of 140 word pairings—one represents "power" and the other represents "force." It is difficult to select just a few, but here is a representative sample of Hawkins's word pairings:

Power	*Force*
Accepting	Rejecting
Allowing	Controlling
Approving	Critical
Believing	Insisting
Choosing to	Having to
Confident	Arrogant
Democratic	Dictatorial
Harmonious	Disruptive
Leading	Coercing

Praising	Flattering
Unifying	Dividing

Here are a few of my own:

Asking	Demanding
Cooperation	Competition
Inviting	Insisting
Open	Resistant
Elective	Requirement
Understanding	Preaching

Every time I try to cajole, push, bully, or otherwise force people or events my way, I usually become frustrated and push people away. When I allow events or people to come to me, I notice that people are happier and things happen with ease. There is no doubt this approach requires more patience. These word pairs are my most powerful reminder to allow things to occur naturally and not force them to happen on my own artificial timetable.

Chapter Four

People Are Paramount

Success is when ordinary people come together to accomplish extraordinary things.

— Steve McNeal, Career Music Educator, Fort Collins, Colorado

Put people first. Most people agree with this dictum. But it's like good taste: Everybody thinks they have it. To some people, putting people first means working hard to be everybody's buddy. There's nothing wrong with being nice. But sometimes, putting people first requires timely communication about your organization's schedule so that a family can make its own plans. Or it can mean making a commitment to train the people in your organization in quality customer service. Or organizing procedures so you don't waste people's time and effort. So, while most people agree in concept, *actions must embody axioms*. In other words, your actions should reflect your values. It's not what you *say*, it's what you *do*. Evaluate policies, processes, and products with consideration for how they affect people. If you really care about people, you will prepare well, follow-through, do what you say you will do, do it truthfully, and do it with a smile.

We try to demonstrate care for the people in the Colorado State University Marching Band by selecting great music, completing the drill designs on time, organizing camp efficiently, and preparing for every rehearsal. We also look out for band members behind the scenes. How much does it cost to be in the band? Do they have comfortable uniforms, quality equipment, and good seats in the stadium? Is the food they are served delicious? (Okay, we could do better there.) How much time do we ask of them? Are

31

they being appreciated, or are they being exploited? If we don't look out for our people, who will? Because other people don't have the total picture, it is up to us to communicate well with decision makers and ensure that band members are cared for.

When I arrived at Colorado State, it was mid July. There had not been a director of bands for fourteen years, so there was plenty to do. Band camp was less than a month away, and I was behind. My to-do list was rapidly filling an entire notepad. As I went through the list, I moved anything related to people to the top. Yes, we still needed to organize the music, show designs, instruments, flags, buses, food, and a myriad of other details. But without the people, there was really no point, because a band is first and foremost "a group of people."

When I started as assistant director of bands at the University of Kentucky, I was twenty-two years old. I thought it was all about the performances. In fact, I didn't bother to learn the name of everyone in the 260-member Wildcat Marching Band. This approach didn't work; I never felt as close to the band as I should have. Consequently, I didn't get the level of commitment from the band that I wanted. Fortunately, Director of Bands Harry Clarke had more knowledge and experience. I began to listen carefully when he said, "It's about people." More importantly, I noticed how he translated the concept into action: leadership retreats, section leader meetings, social events, and communication with band members. But mostly, Mr. Clarke walked into the office every day and got the job done. He chopped wood, carried water, and gave his people a quality product.

It's easy to underestimate the importance of putting people first, especially in regard to your priorities and actions. But this is one of those "ignore at your peril" admonitions. Put people first, take care of relationships, demonstrate that you care through preparation and follow-through, and the performance will take care of itself.

"A" PEOPLE HIRE "A" PEOPLE

One of the most effective ways you can put people first is by having budget priorities that reflect your values. I have noticed over the years that a great band director will create a great band wherever she is. Facilities are important, but a great director can develop a good band with thirteen kids under an apple tree. Following this line of reasoning, when setting the band's budget, we put the staff at the top. Equipment, travel, and food come further down the priority list. We do this because we understand that the quality of the staff is much more important than the quality of the equipment.

If you hire people, hire the very best. Michael Thaut, administrative director of the School of the Arts and former department chair at Colorado State University, helped shape the future of the department through hiring decisions. He states unequivocally that "'A' people hire 'A' people; 'B' people hire 'C' people; 'C' people hire 'D' people; 'D' people hire 'F' people; and 'F' people don't hire." Dr. Thaut goes further: "People hire others of equal ability when they have no issue with their own excellence and know how to seek excellence from others. People hire below their own level of competence when they need to feel superior by having weaker people surrounding themselves. Therefore, hiring a person in a position for which they are not qualified somewhere in a system will eventually bring the system down completely."

Of course, people are not letter grades, and these labels are being used only to quantify a person's ability to excel in a given job. But don't be afraid to hire the very best and expect excellence from them. That's how you will make the grade.

CREATE A "FAMILY"

When you have a family, each person is accepted and loved unconditionally. There is room for everyone. One of the best ways to create a family feeling is to break bread together. In band, we take every opportunity to eat as a group. It's great to start with a giant potluck picnic for the members and their entire families. I also like to bring people into my home. On the first Friday of camp at Colorado State, I invite the entire band over to my house. New members seem surprised at first. But soon, I hope they feel more connected to me as a person and not just a band director— especially after they meet my family, see my children's fingerprints on the windows, and humiliate me in a cutthroat game of foosball.

We try also to create a safe and welcoming environment. We hope people know that it is okay to make mistakes. When I was in high school and working the cleanup shift at an Arby's restaurant, I knocked an expensive bun toaster off the shelf. I am thankful the manager chalked this up as a routine maintenance issue and didn't take it out of my paycheck. One of my band members accidentally ran over her horn in the parking lot; a staff member misplaced an expensive two-way radio; another sideswiped a rental van. Hey, it was all in the line of duty. We can absorb unintentional mistakes because of all the good these people do, most of which is well beyond the call of duty. Most of the time, when a mistake is made, the person more than makes up for it because they care about the organization. People need to feel safe; they need to know that you are going to assume the best about them. It is easier to absorb mistakes when you consider the positive intention behind the action.

THE CHRISTY FACTOR

Veterans in any profession will tell you to be nice to the janitor and the secretary. That starts with not calling them a "janitor" and a "secretary." It's easy to take potshots at "political correctness," but I appreciate the increased sensitivity to calling people by more accurate titles. A custodian is a caretaker, and an executive assistant, administrative assistant, or coordinator has a completely different level of responsibility than a secretary. Learn people's names. The most important word in any person's vocabulary is his or her own name. It is a cop-out to say, "Oh, I'm terrible with names." When you say that, it becomes true. It's okay to say, "Please remind me of your name again," or ask someone else for a reminder. In the Colorado State band, we maintain a yearbook-style picture and name list of every member. It is at rehearsals and available for study at all times. Because 80 percent of learning takes place through review, it is important to review names often. Christy Wiencko (now Muncey) was one of many effective drum majors I have been fortunate to work with. Sometimes, though, I would mangle the pronunciation of her name. Perhaps because of my inconsideration, she made a point of knowing the name of each of the 240 band members by the end of camp week. No doubt, this was a big factor in people feeling welcome and staying with us through some long, hot rehearsals. In fact, we had our largest band ever when Christy was drum major. Coincidence?

Never say anything to someone you wouldn't say in front of their mother.
Say no more.
Everybody is somebody's precious baby.
Think no less.
Catch them doing something right

"Catch them doing something right" is one of the best concepts from *The One Minute Manager* by Kenneth Blanchard and Spencer Johnson. It is easy to find mistakes, and no one is better at it than a band director. But people perform better when they feel good about themselves. This next sentence I write for myself: Look for something to be grateful for—a little appreciation can go a long way. Whenever you praise, be specific and do it publicly. Rather than saying, "That's good," comment on exactly what you think is good. "I love how rich and dark you sound on the last chord," or "Your flanking motions are incredibly sharp." Be sure to find something right with everybody in the group. Compliments to only one section may leave another section feeling underappreciated. If you must criticize, do it privately, and make a sandwich of it. Wrap constructive criticism with positive comments on the top and bottom. Add a little something sweet to make it go down more easily.

I was recently reminded of the power of positive reenforcement during a conducting master class. One of the adult students conducted the professional musicians and received instruction from a "master" teacher. This is a grueling laboratory in which each conducting student bares his or her soul in front of the professors and their fellow students. During this session, "Kathy" had one of those moments when she completely connected with the musicians. The professor complimented her and pointed out that she had achieved one of the most essential fundamentals of conducting—

I remember how receiving a compliment about my playing made me feel so good. I also remember my playing exam for Midwest. I was on the biggest high for the rest of the day because of what was said about me in band. The day after drum major tryouts, it was announced that the three chosen were "captivating." It really made me feel good. There are many other times too, when being in band made me feel special!

—Alyssa Dennison, Lafayette High School Band Member, May 1996

I was sitting in the back in tears as "Kathy" was helped with *O Magnum Mysterium*. That was teaching at its finest. She was boosted with a compliment that was special and honest; she will *never* forget it. She was nurtured and given more confidence and honest instruction than I've seen in a very long time—and I'm surrounded by wonderful educators. This is the kindness and care in instruction that I aspire to. That moment has made the entire three-year program worth it for me.

—Sarah Harrison, Choral Director, Cherry Creek High School, July 2009

communication. She savored the moment and became more receptive to detailed instruction. The following letter reveals the impact of "catching them doing something right," not only on the person who is "caught" but also on all those who witness it.

MR. MOORE TO THE PRINCIPAL'S OFFICE

Remember the pit in your stomach when you were called to the principal's office? It's even worse when you're an adult! One Saturday morning at six, the Lafayette High School Band was loaded on five buses and headed off to compete in the 1996 Kentucky State Marching Band Championships. I felt a lot of pressure to defend the title, which we had won for five straight years. My head chaperone and I brought some coffee on the bus, but the driver told me it was not allowed. I corrected him and told him that it *was* allowed as long as the bus was not moving. This led to a battle of wills, which ended in me getting the last word: "Well, you don't have to be an ass about it." The bus full of teenagers got very quiet. For the rest of the trip, the bus driver, for some reason, could never seem to get us to the correct location. At one point, I stopped all of the buses and asked 237 students to walk across a field to make sure we were on time for our warm-up. On Monday morning, I got a note in my school mailbox: "Please stop by the principal's office." I was pretty sure this was not to congratulate me on our sixth state championship. As I sat across from Principal Thurmas Reynolds, I noticed a letter from the school system's transportation department in his hands. Mr. Reynolds looked at me:

"Says here you called the bus driver a *name* on Saturday," he said.

"Yes, sir," I replied hesitantly. "I did."

"Hmm," he said with a long pause. "Well, was he acting like one?"

"Well, yes, I thought so," I replied with a slight tremor in my voice.

The principal thought for a moment, ripped the letter in half, and said, "Okay, that's good enough for me." I immediately apologized and assured him that it would never happen again.

When I left the office, I was relieved that I had not been officially reprimanded, and I was determined to act more professionally in the future. Mr. Reynolds had a much bigger effect on me by *not* scolding me. I would have gone to the wall for that principal if he ever needed it—not that he ever did. I try to remember that incident when people have temporary lapses in judgment. Sometimes people don't need criticism as much as they need compassion, and the problem will correct itself.

WATCH YOUR GARDEN BLOOM

I love how the band experience helps develop people's confidence. Band directors are usually good at seeing potential in people. Greg Byrne, the University of Louisville's band director, certainly saw potential in Patrick Henry Hughes. Now, Patrick's book is appropriately titled *I Am Potential*. Imagine your group as a garden and all of the members as flowers. Some need a little more water than others, some need a little more light, and all of them need care and feeding. There is nothing more rewarding than watching people bloom. Of course, some flowers bloom quickly, and some need more coaxing. But a good gardener knows the difference.

One of my beautiful clarinetists, Kimberly Henderson, came to the band with an insecure habit of covering her mouth when she smiled. It reminded me of Celie, the protagonist in the movie *The Color Purple*. But Kimberly was well nourished in the band's soil, and she added much to the grandeur of our garden. She could flat-out play any technical passage you put in front of her. In 1999, several years after Kimberly's graduation, I was called to jury duty in downtown Lexington, Kentucky. Imagine my pleasure at seeing Ms. Henderson, attorney-at-law, walk confidently into the courtroom, notice me, and flash a smile as if to say, "Look at me, I'm no wallflower now!"

NEVER GIVE UP ON PEOPLE

Never give up on people. Always leave the door open for your people, even if they may not appear to be meeting expectations. Some people have a longer fuse than others. With patience, you may be surprised at how they will "catch fire" later on. Sometimes, you must be willing to absorb some behaviors that are not ideal. But this almost always pays dividends in the long run.

Alethea Devary was one of those people who wasn't afraid to question "the system." Most of the time, band members think of me *as* the system, so they naturally assume that I don't appreciate people who question authority. Truth is, I like it—unless they question *my* authority. But, seriously, I like it when someone cares enough to ask questions and challenge policy. Most bureaucratic systems need improvement, and a rebellious streak is sometimes necessary for success. Although Alethea did her share of bucking the system, she was a stellar performer in the marching band. Unfortunately, she wasn't as successful elsewhere in school. I was disappointed when she didn't graduate from Lafayette, but my faith in her was rewarded later when she sent me a letter with her GED (high-school equivalency diploma) attached. It showed a lot of heart for her to share these feelings with me.

I realize I put you through nothing but pure hell over the years. Nevertheless, I have a great deal of respect for you. Band was the only class I truly enjoyed. You are the only teacher that has had an impact on me and actually influenced me and taught me things. I disappointed you, myself, and many others by messing up in school, but I recently received my GED and just last Tuesday applied to Lexington Community College and financial aid. I thought you might like to see a copy of my (GED) scores.

—Alethea Devary, Lafayette High School Band Member, May 1996

You bet I wanted to see her scores! I also read her letter to the band. I was proud of Alethea's achievement. All of her scores were high, but my heart warmed when I noticed her highest scores were in Interpreting Literature and the Arts. Alethea has more than 130 credit hours from the University of Kentucky, a great job, and she is an amazingly creative photographer. She still maintains her individuality, and I respect her for it.

IT'S NOT THE YEARS

On the occasion of the fiftieth anniversary of the Central Kentucky Youth Orchestra, we invited past conductors to return for a celebratory concert. It was the first time I had met Marvin Rabin, an internationally renowned authority in string music education. I was surprised at his youthful vitality because I knew he conducted the orchestra in the early 1950s. However, I noticed crevasses around his eyes and mouth. They had become deep, permanent features. When Dr. Rabin rehearsed the ensemble, the source of his wrinkles immediately became clear. He smiled warmly at each and every one of the orchestra's musicians throughout the entire rehearsal. Decades of smiling at thousands of musicians had revealed itself as laugh lines on the face of a caring maestro. Whenever the issue of age comes up, I am fond of saying, "It's not the years, it's the miles." However, Maestro Rabin's example teaches us, "It's not the years, it's the *smiles*."

MARCHING TO THE BEAT OF
A DIFFERENT DRUM MAJOR

Sometimes, it is important to do what's better for the individual than the group. I once guilted Doug Bratt into playing trombone in the Lafayette Band instead of his first love, percussion. I figured that we needed low-brass players a lot more than drummers, and what's good for the band would be good for Doug. He was disappointed but good natured about it. Now I can hear him laughing every time he sends me news of his latest recordings and concert reviews as a professional drummer in Chicago.

Thankfully, the late George Parks's band director had more compassion than I did. George was the director of the Minuteman Marching Band at the University of Massachusetts and the world's preeminent teacher of drum majors. He actually wrote *the* book on it, and he trained more than 75,000 people in the art of field conducting and leadership. And it all happened because his band director, L. Jerome Rehberg, allowed his all-state tuba player to become the drum major of the Christiana Senior High School Viking Band of Newark, Delaware.

LED DOWN THE GARDEN PATH

Decisions such as this can work both ways. Craig Cornish is now the renowned director of the Middle Tennessee State University Band of Blue. Even though he was the best clarinetist in the Lafayette Band at the time, my father asked him to play sousaphone in the marching band. He agreed, and now he is one of the finest brass instructors in the business. It may be that, as a member of an organization, a person is asked to do something that is outside his comfort zone. In those situations, an appropriate response might be, "I'm happy to do whatever is best for the group."

Conversely, leaders may have to make decisions that, *at the time*, appear to be more desirable for the individual than for the organization. And often, the consequence is surprisingly better for everyone. No matter how well designed, a garden is only as beautiful as its individual flowers. If every flower is healthy and well nurtured, you have a better chance at having a gorgeous garden. Some flowers just need the right soil in which to thrive.

In a membership role, be open to doing what is best for the group, even if it represents a change for you. In a leadership role, don't force anyone, and be sensitive to individuals' desires. By the way, we need more sousaphone players in our band this fall. Anyone interested?

EVERY LIVING SOUL

I hope you agree by now that while product is prominent, people are priority. The means is always as important as the end. The way you do things is as important as the things you do. In the long run, this will result in a stronger, more sustainable organization. Ben Hawkins, music professor at Transylvania University in Lexington, Kentucky, is one of my trusted colleagues and longtime friends. He shared a quote with me that I wish I had read at the beginning of my career:

> Accepting life whole and keeping one's love of art from idolatry means remembering that non-living things must be loved soberly. The living have first claim.

> —Jacques Barzun, *Toward a Fateful Serenity*

Chapter Five

Leadership Lessons

There's no such thing as a bad band, just bad band directors.

—J. Larry Moore

THE MAN IN THE MIRROR

I hate it when he says that—"There's no such thing as a bad band, just bad band directors." I call home looking for *support,* not blame. My dad was a band director, surely he should understand. It's not my fault. The situation is intolerable, and people just aren't doing what they are supposed to be doing. In fact, it's not only ridiculous—*it is an injustice!* Clearly, I have done all I can do. If only you had heard it. They're just not practicing. I'm not sure they even *care.* I can't be expected to work miracles.

"Well, I'm sorry, son, but you need to look in the mirror," Dad replied. "There's no such thing as a bad band, just bad band directors."

When we get to this point in the conversation, I don't want to admit that I might be at fault. The problem is, I later realize that he is right, I am wrong, and there is something else I should have been doing.

Sometimes, it takes me *years* to figure out things, and that really hurts. I began rehearsal every day for ten years with Bach's Chorale no. 12, arranged by Matthew Lake. It frustrated me to no end when people miscounted a simple half note in this chorale. What is wrong with people that they can't count 1-2? During my doctoral studies, Professor David MacKenzie introduced me to the concept of using a completely horizontal gesture during a passive beat, such as beat two of a half note. The next time I conducted the chorale, no one miscounted the half note. My elation was tempered considerably by the knowledge that all of these years the problem wasn't bad counting, just bad conducting.

THE MORE YOU FOCUS ON OTHERS,
THE BETTER IT BECOMES FOR YOU

There are plenty of other examples of my bad band directing I could have chosen, but I selected this one because many of the others still sting. I've mentioned that I didn't get to know the students well enough in my first bands at the University of Kentucky. During my first few years at Lafayette, I didn't teach fundamentals as well as I should have. I *did* fundamentals; I just didn't *teach* them. Most of the time I said the right things, but I didn't connect with the band members in a way that they truly heard me. Because communication is a two-way activity, you don't communicate if others aren't listening. I was too concerned with proving myself. I made sure that everyone knew I had experience with drum and bugle corps and college bands, so they should listen to me and let me lead them to glory. Unfortunately, I wasn't listening to the band members enough. My leadership was more concerned with my goals rather than understanding their needs—thus, we didn't communicate. When it became more about "we," the band members' leadership was allowed to flourish. Ironically, the less it was about "me" the better it became for me. All of *their* accomplishments looked good on *my* resume.

THE STICK-A DON'T MAKE-A DA MUSIC

"The stick-a don't make-a da music." I heard a military band conductor make this statement once in a pseudo-Italian accent. Now, I can't think of it any other way. That's not important, but it does lead to a noteworthy realization for a conductor: *You don't make any sound.* The woodwinds, brass, percussion, strings, and vocalists create the vibrations that reverberate through the air and are received by the audience members' ears and go straight to their hearts. The conductor doesn't even face the audience! When the conductor takes the stage and asks the performers to stand, it's to acknowledge that the applause is for the musicians. At the conclusion of a concert, the conductor recognizes the individual soloists, then the entire ensemble; he takes a bow on behalf of the musicians and then gives it up to them by turning toward the ensemble and gesturing to the players with open body language. It's the people in the ensemble who make the music.

Now, conductors still have vital functions: They choose the music, recruit the players, plan the rehearsals, teach the concepts, schedule the concerts, promote the performances, administer the ensemble, and work with heart and soul to inspire passion in the performers. Conductors serve as musical historian, theorist, counselor, psychologist, mentor, and friend. Conductors sculpt the sound; they ask the performers to breathe and play together in the same manner in which their hands move up and down. Conductors show the music with the way they move: float, glide, flick, dab, punch, slash, press, and wring. Shorter, longer, faster, slower, louder, softer. They move toward a musical moment or move away from it. Conductors set the tempo and adjust the speed to match the ability of the players, the reverberation time of the hall, and even the emotional contour of the performance. Conductors encourage the players, cue the entrances, time the releases, and demonstrate the dynamics. Conductors illuminate the music to the performers *and* the audience by visually representing its mood and style through gestures, facial expression, and body language. A great conductor *is* the music. The music flows through the conductor like a source of energy: first the breath, then the nose, mouth, eyes, eyebrows, arms, hands, fingers, spine, abdomen, legs, and feet. Even the hair! It's true: The hair moves with the music. The composer conceives the music, but the conductor breathes life into it and delivers it to the world. Conceive it, believe it, achieve it. So, there is no reason to diminish the role of the conductor, a job people give their lives to. But a conductor must know his role. A conductor, like a great leader, is the catalyst to a creative process that results in the uplifting of mankind. But in the end, the conductor doesn't make any sound, and he gives all of the recognition to the people who do. In fact, if a conductor does his job really well, the ensemble can play without him—breathing and moving together, taking cues from each other, and absorbing all of the good vibrations sent back in the form of applause. The better the leader, the more the musicians face the audience, make the music, and receive the appreciation.

With this in mind, the less you are noticed, the more effect you have. If you are in the spotlight too much, you need to adjust the lighting. If it ever becomes apparent that you are not receiving recognition for a job well done, it may be that you did your job exceedingly well. Take a breath and enjoy the moment; there are enough good vibrations in the hall for everybody.

SERVICE LEADERSHIP

Band leadership has changed considerably during the past sixty years. It has reflected a shift in society, and the evolution has been positive for everyone concerned. Because a lot of marching band processes came from the military, there is a heritage of top-down management. Add to that the influence from the orchestral world of the all-powerful maestro—think of the famously temperamental Arturo Toscanini—and you have a volatile mix of power and arrogance. Some band directors routinely declare: "This is *not* a democracy—it is a dictatorship." There are famous stories describing musicians so humiliated by a conductor that they put their instrument in its case and never got it out again. I once saw a girl get so frustrated from being singled out during a rehearsal that she took the clarinet she was playing, broke it over her knee, and walked out. (It wouldn't have been so bad if the clarinet had belonged to her instead of my buddy, Craig Cornish!) But the old ways have changed; good band directors now embrace more of a service style of leadership.

Style has changed in part because of the influence of Dr. W. Edwards Deming, the American leadership guru who revolutionized the Japanese automobile industry. Top-down management has been turned upside down. In the new paradigm, the leader is an encourager, a recognizer of potential, a possibility thinker, a cocreator, and a visionary—but not just of his own vision. He works in synergy with the administration, the community, and the group to develop a harmonious stream of well-being that flows through the organization. In a college band model, the band director serves the staff, which often consists of an administrative assistant, graduate assistants, a percussion instructor, and auxiliary instructors. The director and staff serve the drum majors and section leaders. The drum majors and section leaders serve the band members. The band members serve the community. The community supports the university. The university supports the administration. The administration supports the departments. The departments support the band director. And the cycle is sustained.

The service-oriented leadership paradigm is noticeably successful in bands. It has been developed through the leadership training workshops, books, and role model of Dr. Tim Lautzenheiser. It isn't possible or necessary for me to summarize his teachings, although I encourage you to read his materials. Instead, I would like to share some examples of band members who taught me valuable leadership lessons.

DO YOU WANT TO LEAD, OR DO YOU WANT THE TITLE?

Elizabeth Brady (now Witherspoon) was an outstanding student at Lafayette from an incredible family. She was a leader in several organizations. She was so bright and such a fabulous clarinetist that I often was challenged to challenge her. She was selected as the drum major of what turned out to be our first championship band—probably no coincidence there. She was nominated to Youth Salute, a prestigious program that recognizes and encourages leadership. The program selected students from around the state who held leadership positions in at least two organizations. The students received various recognitions, including a portrait display that toured major shopping malls in Kentucky. The program culminated in a weekend leadership conference and awards program. The winner received a scholarship to the Kentucky school of his or her choice and a lot of publicity.

I got word that Liz was going to be the winner. I was excited, imagining the publicity it would bring to the band and, of course, to me! The only hitch was that she had to be present at the awards banquet to receive the award. As fate would have it, the banquet was at the same time as our big competition in a nearby town. In disbelief, I suggested everything from changing the rules to hiring a helicopter to fly her from the competition to the banquet, none of which was acceptable to the awards committee. The choice came down to this: Be crowned Youth Salute Leader of the Year and not be present to lead her group, or be the leader of her group in action and relinquish the title. I was upset and unsure about what I thought she should do. I wanted this title for her, because she deserved it, and I selfishly wanted the acclaim for our band. Her parents and I brought the issue to Liz. Without the slightest hesitation, she said, "Of course, I will be at the band contest. No question about it." She never blinked, and she didn't even seem to be disappointed. She was unequivocal in her commitment to the group that had selected her as its leader. She led the band that evening, and another deserving person received the award. And, by the way, the next year she went to Yale University.

LEADERSHIP LESSONS FROM
A FOURTEEN-YEAR-OLD

I met Tyler Stevens at Picadome Elementary School in Lexington, Kentucky. He joined the beginning band class and showed considerable talent as a trumpet player. He certainly had a great attitude. Tyler stole my heart at the end of the year. Most Picadome kids went to Beaumont Middle School and, for a number of reasons, Beaumont kids rarely went on to join the Lafayette Band at that time. So you can imagine how nice it was to hear Tyler say, "I can't wait to go to Lafayette and wear the Lafayette Band uniform." Bull's-eye: straight to my heart. You have me, kid. As a Lafayette Band alumnus, I felt the same way about the uniform; I was always proud to wear it. "Awesome, Tyler! I will see you in three years."

And so I did. Now taller than me, Tyler joined the band. But at a trumpet section rehearsal at band camp, I was disappointed by his playing. Every note he played began with a blip, the kind you get when your fingers don't move in sync with your tongue. Of course, I was quick to point this out.

"Tyler, you sounded better than that in the fifth grade!" I said, prompting him to break down in tears.

"I am trying the best I can!" he said. "I don't know what's wrong!"

Okay, so I didn't get Teacher of the Year honors for that exchange, but I made a quick recovery and we journeyed on.

As camp continued, the veterans and I began our indoctrination into the total commitment and dedication expected for marching band. "We *never* march with an absence," I preached. "Unless you are phoning in from your own funeral, you will be at every performance and pretty much every rehearsal. We've had people perform with (insert all manner of ailments here). This is Lafayette, and we *have always* and we *will always* march with a full band." Everybody drank the Kool-Aid.

The weekend of the first contest approached, and we were rehearsing hard on the pavement that Tuesday after school. No one missed rehearsal the week of the first contest, especially without a phone call. But Tyler was absent. Because attitude was never an issue with him, I knew something must be wrong. Sure enough, I got word that Tyler was in the hospital. Fingers and tongue not working together. Brain tumor. My heart sank. Assistant Director Terry Magee and I went to visit Tyler in the hospital. He was upbeat when we asked how he was doing.

"Great!" he said. "You know the band parent Miss Walters? She's a nurse on this floor. She's bringing me all the food and cookies I want! See that giant card? That's from the trumpet section! And the balloons; the entire band sent those! Yeah, I'm having surgery Friday and I know it will all be okay."

Then, a little more softly, he said, "Mr. Moore, I'm sorry about the contest Saturday. I know you never march with an absence, but I'm not going to be able to be there with my surgery and all."

I got that sickening feeling that happens when you know you said it and wish you could take it back. "Tyler, it's fine," I said. "You have a great reason."

"Okay, Mr. Moore, but please tell the band I will be there with them in spirit," Tyler said. "I'll be back to school soon and marching in the band."

Here Tyler is, facing brain surgery, and he's thinking about the welfare of the band. I would have been cursing God and asking, "Why me?" I left the hospital thinking about the lesson I had just gotten from a fourteen-year-old about putting other people first. From then on, I toned down the "never march with an absence" speech. Well, a little.

We marched the show that Saturday, and I think the kids wore armbands in solidarity with Tyler. We did it with the hole in the forms, but I quickly filled it the next week. It was an emotional show: highlights from *Les Misérables*. The band started camp with a trip to Nashville, Tennessee, to experience the musical. The band performed the show with all of the commitment I could ever hope for. The season was progressing well, and we were poised to win our fifth straight Contest of Champions, which would be unprecedented. I never imagined Tyler would be in that show, but one day, as promised, he knocked on my door.

"I'm back and I'm ready to march!" Tyler said, a bandana around his head to cover the incision. High school kids can be cruel, but not this group. I wasn't sure what to do with him, but Terry Magee said he had a plan. We gave Tyler a new role, and he practiced it every day as if it were the most important role ever. He ran a massive red flag across the field, just like in the musical, and waved it in a legato figure eight at the climax of the show. As the last chord rang out—and band members were playing their hearts out—Tyler stood at attention front and center, proud to wear the Lafayette Band uniform.

It doesn't matter who won the contest that year. I remember Tyler, and it still makes my heart sing. He became a section leader, and later I shared a commencement ceremony with him at the University of Kentucky. I got a conducting degree, and he got a science degree. He's now enriching the lives of students as an assistant professor at Virginia Commonwealth University.

RICH THE CHEERLEADER

Some people are vocal leaders; some are leaders by example. Rich Alphin was both.

I hate it when people miss band camp. In fact, I don't guarantee them a spot in the show unless they attend camp. Fortunately, few miss. But Rich did. To make matters worse, his parents insisted he go with them to Hawaii while we were pounding the pavement in humid central Kentucky. He also drove a white Mercedes-Benz convertible. I thought he might be too spoiled to be a member of our band. Give me blue-collar kids with a work ethic and I will show you a band that won't quit. But we put Rich in the show. He played tuba and, well, there is always a spot for someone willing to carry a sousaphone.

Have you ever seen one of those people who can't tap their toe or put their feet down in time with the music? A lot of big kids are like that when they first join marching band. There's just too much going on with the breathing and the tonguing and the fingering and the watching and the turning and the marching. But we were pretty good at fixing those problems, especially if a kid had a can-do attitude. Rich did, and more. He was enthusiastic and told me, "I'm sorry I'm late, but I'm going to come early and stay late to work with the section leader. I am going to get this, you'll see!" He made a believer out of me, and the next year he was the section leader.

There's always a lot of "let's go back and do it one more time" in marching band. In almost any band, you will hear a whiny chorus of "Aaahhh" whenever the director says, "Just one more time." But Rich would drown out everyone with his enthusiasm. He would *race* back to position, fifty pounds of twisted brass and all, crying out, "All right! Let's do it!" He even had *me* running back. You know, it only takes one positive person to sway an entire group.

As we approached the Contest of Champions performance, we went through our normal precontest ritual of inspecting all instruments and uniforms. This is a holdover from the old days, when inspections were part of the contest. I figured that at least once a year everybody's instrument and uniform should be in perfect condition, so why not pick a day and have it all perfect at the same time? Every horn slide worked, brass shone, woodwind pads were new, mouthpieces were clean, dents were repaired, uniforms were perfect, shoes were tied the same way, and everyone stood at perfect attention while I went down the line inspecting each and every person. Yeah, Kool-Aid time again. But this was serious business and one of the reasons we were a great band. We took pride in perfection, and no detail was deemed too small to be significant.

So, you might imagine my shock when I found a four-inch dent in Rich's horn, just under his right elbow. Even though he was much taller than me, he stammered when he tried to explain that the dent was caused by the force with which the sousaphone section flanked (made a quick turn) during the show. In fact, he claimed that all of the sousaphones had them. You see, the band executed a very sharp turn that happened in a split second. It was like a camera flash. One moment, band members faced the end zone; the next, they faced ninety degrees to the right. The sousaphone section had perfected this turn, and it added much effect to the show when those big bells caught the stadium lights. I protested that it was impossible to dent the thick metal of a sousaphone with just the force of a flank. So I went down the line. He was right; every instrument had the same four-inch dent in exactly the same place. That day, an exception was made in the Lafayette inspection protocol: We left the sousaphone dents as a badge of honor.

The next fall, the Symphonic Band (our indoor concert band) was invited to play at the Midwest International Band and Orchestra Clinic. This is perhaps the highest honor a high school band can achieve. Only five bands worldwide are chosen to play. The Midwest is a clinic for band and orchestra directors, so the entire audience is filled with musicians who know music and know bands. They either love you or hate you. If you're good, no crowd will appreciate it more than this one. If not, well, let's just say that there are plenty of other things to do in Chicago. That day we were feeling it pretty good, and the audience was right there with us. We closed the concert with Giuseppe Verdi's *La Forza del Destino,* the "Forces of Destiny." The woodwinds were knocking out the exposed technical lines with crystal-clear perfection. The emotional energy emanating from the band was palpable. As we were coming down the homestretch and nearing the coda, I got ready to give a big cue to the tubas. Rich, in his excitement, came in a measure too early—loudly. Oh well, there was nothing I could do about it then. We finished the piece in a burst of sonic exuberance, and the crowd responded in solidarity.

Our band members stood up and soaked in the applause like a big sponge. I will never forget the enthusiastic ovation. As the applause died down, I looked over at Rich. His head was down and he was looking hangdog. I went over to him and put my arm around his shoulder.

"I've ruined the concert," he said in a breaking voice, tears in his eyes.

"No, Rich," I replied. "You made the concert. We never would have been on this stage without you, buddy. You carried us here on your broad shoulders."

I don't know if I said every word of that, but I think he got the message. Now, when I listen to that recording, the early entrance of one tuba sounds pretty good to my ear.

THIS ONE TIME, AT BOOT CAMP . . .

Earlier in this chapter I discussed the idea that leadership is most successful when it is allowed to come naturally from within the group. In other words, a genuine leader doesn't dictate but serves the membership in such a way that each person is empowered to give his or her personal best. Many successful directors have been known to say, "This is your band, not mine." As in a democracy, ownership of the ensemble is of the people, by the people, and for the people. How American is that?

I was reminded of this principle when I attended a recent reunion of Lafayette Band members from the years I was their director. Former trumpet player Peter Kasarskis used the occasion to share some of his memories about the band. Now, most would agree that Peter knows something about leadership. As a captain in the U.S. Air Force, he trains our nation's elite fighter pilots. He has six-hundred-plus combat hours supporting ground troops in combat zones. Let's just say I am pleased that someone of his intelligence and ability is helping to keep our country safe.

As one might expect, Peter learned a great deal about leadership, self-discipline, and striving for perfection at the U.S. Air Force Academy in Colorado Springs, Colorado. But he is quick to credit his experience in the Lafayette Band as having planted the seeds for those leadership traits. I've heard from other former students that they were well prepared for the military as a result of their experience in the Lafayette Band. It is often expressed as, "Boot camp was nothing compared to band camp!" Many a truth is said in jest.

In the following reflection, Peter explains the importance of membership and the value of leadership that comes from within the ranks.

My proudest moment in the band? When I was younger I might have said that it was a contest we barely won against a strong rival, or playing with Allen Vizutti and Vince DiMartino at the Midwest convention, or perhaps hearing the crowd during the 1994 state marching finals. All were special, memorable moments never to be forgotten.

But as an adult, I have a different response. In my final year, the music and drill were exceptionally difficult. The band had fallen behind in combining the music with the drill, yet no practices had been scheduled during a holiday weekend. Unbeknownst to the directors, the student leaders decided to rehearse on Labor Day to catch up.

The plan was announced without the directors. It was presented as, "If you already have plans, that's fine, but if you don't, the band could greatly benefit from an extra rehearsal." Much to our surprise only four or five of more than 250 students were unable to attend. It started on time, and the drum majors led the band in fundamentals, warm-ups, and rehearsal without a hitch. It was an incredible display of leadership from the drum majors, assertive "followership" from other senior leaders in support, and dedication from everyone else.

Evidently, Mr. Moore learned of the plan and showed up late in the rehearsal. He stood on the sidelines without interrupting and observed something truly amazing. In what other organization can you see such discipline, leadership, and selflessness emerge?

So, that is my proudest band moment—no crowd, no glamour, just being part of a group of people who were dedicated to something bigger than themselves. In a "me-first" society, that was special.

—Captain Peter Kasarskis, Former Lafayette Band Member, July 2009

Chapter Six

Individual Responsibility

If everyone in the band were like me, how would the band be?

—Tim Lautzenheiser

ONE FLY IN THE PUNCH BOWL

Music often includes moments of silence that are vital to the composition. Early in the rehearsal process of preparing for a concert, invariably someone will play during a rest. If this happens more than once, I invoke the phrase, "It's just one fly in the punch bowl! Don't you want to drink the punch? It has just got one fly in it!" Since I am usually much too serious in rehearsal, this juvenile aphorism often elicits giggles and groans. But I think musicians get the idea that it only takes one flaw to ruin it for everybody. Each person has an individual responsibility to keep the punch bowl clean. And nobody wants to be called an insect!

REHEARSAL IS WHERE YOU DO THAT
WHICH CAN'T BE DONE ALONE

If you care about others, you prepare before rehearsal. Don't come to a meeting unprepared. If everyone is individually prepared, the group has an opportunity to achieve a much higher level of excellence.

THE DEFINITION OF SUCCESS

Vince DiMartino was my trumpet teacher throughout high school and again for a couple of years as an adult. Although Vince is only a few years older than I am, he was a musical prodigy and began performing professionally at a young age. He is of Italian heritage and embodies the greatest characteristics of that culture. He is a musician to the core of his being, and he has a love of people that effortlessly bubbles to the surface. During lessons, he used to pinch my cheeks and say, "Stevie, you gotta be smart to be a musician! Use your brain!" It's the first time I realized that intelligence and music were connected. Vince was way ahead of Harvard psychologist Howard Gardner, who wrote in his landmark book, *Frames of Mind,* that music is an intelligence. Vince is recognized as one of the world's finest trumpeters. He is one of those rare people who is not only an incredible performer but also loves to teach. He taught me much about music, so it is somewhat embarrassing to share this simple saying as representative of what I learned from him, but I'm not going to let that stop me because I'm not that smart.

The definition of success is the ability to meet deadlines.

When I first heard this, I thought it was a shallow statement. Surely there is much more to success than meeting a few deadlines. What about intelligence, talent, luck, timing, and hard work? But, over the decades, I have come to appreciate the unfailing accuracy of this definition. I went to graduate school at the University of Kentucky beginning at the age of thirty-eight. As an adult student, I was able to take a more disciplined approach to my studies and class preparations than I did as a teenager. From the beginning, I decided to attend every class with all the readings and homework completed. In meeting these incremental deadlines, I met the overall goal of achieving a doctor of musical arts in just a few years. More importantly, I actually *learned* from the classes rather than just getting good grades.

Recently I served on a Colorado State University search committee to hire an associate director of bands. Committee members wanted to complete the search by the end of the fall semester. We worked backward in time from the goal date and set incremental deadlines. Committee members appreciated the efficiency and clarity of the time line, and the process ran with precision. We made an offer to a tremendously talented musician, Chris Nicholas, the last week of the semester. Soon, all of the paperwork was complete, and he returned his signed contract. Not two days later, all searches in our college were shut down in anticipation of budget cuts. Because we had a contract in place, our hire was spared. We now have a great band director because of our simple ability to meet deadlines.

Alternatively, time and again I have known people who fail because they can't meet deadlines. Again, it is usually incremental: not just one project that is late but a series of small failures to meet deadlines that accumulate over time. At some point, the weight of the failure is out of balance with the desire to succeed, and the person gives up. When you decide you want to achieve a goal, it is important to set up a system or path to achieve the goal and apply a time line. Where are you compared to where you want to be? How can you move incrementally from point A to point B? Set up a timetable and chart a path to success. Check off each increment and celebrate your progress. Meet each deadline, and you are guaranteed success.

BAR BY BAR, YOU CAN BE A STAR

Sometimes the best approach to a task is to take it incrementally. You can't eat an entire veggie burger in one bite. When encouraging band members to memorize their music, at some point I will say, "Bar by bar, you can be a star." (Just to be clear: This is a reference to a measure of music, not a drinking establishment.) This is a takeoff on the motivational author Rev. Robert Schuller's axiom, "Inch by inch, anything's a cinch." Breaking down any task into manageable parts allows it to become possible. Because most people agree that the first step is the most difficult, step off by breaking the task down into logical increments. And don't spend too much time in bars.

YOU SHALL DO WHAT YOU SAY YOU SHALL DO

We had a great minister at the church I attended in Lexington, Kentucky. The Rev. Kelly Flood was a fabulous role model for group leaders, and

I tried to learn as much as possible from her. Some might say I learned more at church about band directing than I did about religion, but that's another story. There were many requests to volunteer for projects at church, but she made it clear that it was always okay to say no. I appreciated that understanding and have adopted the same creed in my bands. That way, I don't feel guilty about asking for help. So, it's okay to say no; but it's a sin to say you will do something and then not follow-through, even if you have a good reason. Along with permission to say no, you are forgiven if you speak up later because you cannot complete the task. Just do it as soon as possible so another willing soul can take over.

MUSICIANS' TIME

How do you know a drummer is knocking at your door? The knocking rushes. That old joke doesn't actually make sense because percussionists have the best time of anyone in band. (Yes, you caught the double entendre.) Band members in general operate on a different time schedule. Ask my former students what they learned in band, and you will likely hear this quote attributed to the legendary coach Vince Lombardi:

> To be early is to be on time. To be on time is to be late.

But this version has more edge, and truth, for anyone who ever showed up late for a band trip:

> To be early is to be on time. To be on time is to be late. To be late is to be left.

Of course, if for some reason a band member misses the bus at the beginning of a trip, he is still expected to find his way to the destination. If there is a performance involved, he will walk, bike, drive, or hitchhike to get to the show on time. (I once convinced a South Carolina state trooper to give me a ride through game-day traffic to make it to the stadium on time.) Band members show up, and they show up on time. They do it because they care enough about each other and the good of the group. This basic consideration carries over to all aspects of life. This is a continuation of the basic band tenet that everyone is important. Once on a band trip, everybody knows that the bus can't leave until everybody is on it.

It never ceases to amaze me how cooperative a group of band members can be. I recently took five buses and a truck to the New Mexico Bowl. The trip included a traveling party of 240 band members, two graduate assistants, one band coordinator, and me. There was a complex, intense schedule of rehearsals and performances, but everything went as smoothly as a German train schedule. If you want a great employee, hire a former band member. And don't forget to be early for the first meeting.

SHOW UP

Band members do more than show up on time; you can count on them to show up no matter the circumstance. Tricia Hampton (now Cary) as a junior played principal (first chair) clarinet in the symphonic band. Tricia was an accomplished musician, but she was also admired for an impassioned speech she gave to the school board as an eighth grader to save the music program. On the way to the last concert of the year, as well as my last concert as director of the Lafayette Band, Tricia was in a serious car accident. Immediately after being released from the hospital, she came to the Lexington Opera House in a neck brace. Knowing that she was vital to the performance (as are all of the performers), she insisted on playing. Dr. Edward Sames, a former band member and my best friend, was asked to check her. While he didn't think it was necessarily the best idea for her to play, he recognized the look of determination in her eyes. He decided that

At the spring concert when I was hurt, I never thought I was going to make it through the whole performance, but looking up at you conducting and knowing that it would be the last time I would ever play for you, I was able to keep going. It really helped me feel better knowing that you were there, making sure that I was doing all right. I really appreciate you going out of your way to call and make sure I was better on Friday. I'm so lucky to have a teacher who cares for me and all his students so much.

—Tricia Hampton, Lafayette High School Band Member, May 1996 the disappointment of not playing would cause more harm that the physical stress of performing. I was thankful—and moved. When you have loyalty to the group, you can rise above individual pain. When people are willing to make any sacrifice for the good of the group, you know you have something special. That's a group I want to be part of.

CHECKLIST FOR SUCCESS

When I was the band director at Lafayette High School and Jessie Clark Middle School, my talented team teacher, Cynthia Hawkins, and I routinely published a "checklist for success." We touted this list as a proven plan for success as a music student:

1. A positive attitude and encouraging parents
2. Good attendance at school and practices
3. *Private lessons*
4. Have a professional-quality instrument
5. Audition for honor bands and all-state bands
6. Play a solo or duet at contest each year
7. Attend summer music camps
8. Practice five days a week, twenty to forty minutes a day
9. Have good recordings of artists on your instrument
10. Attend band, orchestra, and professional soloist concerts

I think this is a good list for success in any endeavor. Here's why:

1. *A positive attitude and encouraging parents.* No. 1 on any list is a positive attitude. Skills and knowledge are important, but experience and research show the importance of attitude. You also need the support of your family and loved ones.
2. *Good attendance at school and practices.* We have already discussed showing up, but it is worth repeating. Take care of yourself and be healthy. It takes twice as much effort to miss a day and make it up as it does to be there in the first place.
3. **Private lessons.** Notice that taking private lessons is in bold type. That's because I want to emphasize its importance; it's like an insurance

policy for success. If you truly want to excel, it is important to spend one-on-one time with the best teacher or consultant you can find.

4. *Have a professional-quality instrument.* Whatever your field, own the best equipment you can afford. Don't work with inferior tools. You can't tune a bad piano, and you can't win a car race in a clunker. I agree with the truck commercials that urge you to choose "professional grade."

5. *Audition for honor bands and all-state bands.* Look for the "honor" organizations in your field. There is always room at the top, so make it a goal to be in the top 10 percent of your profession. The continual effort to improve your knowledge, skill, and attitude will keep you challenged and help you avoid professional stagnation.

6. *Play a solo or duet at contest each year.* Apply to present at a symposium in your area of expertise, or increase your ability by performing alone or in a small group whose work is judged. Not only will you see how you compare with others but also you will improve your skills and understanding through assessment. Finding a public exhibition or performance for your work provides motivation and puts you on a deadline.

7. *Attend summer music camps.* Find time to recharge and have some fun interacting with others in your profession. The camaraderie will buoy your spirit and provide fresh approaches to your challenges. It is great to get away and enjoy a new environment. The distance can help provide a perspective on your situation.

8. *Practice five days a week, twenty to forty minutes a day.* Improve your skills daily. What is the most important action you can take to become better at your job? What one action would make the most difference in your success if you did it daily for a few minutes? Prioritize and schedule it like a meeting you can't miss.

9. *Have good recordings of artists on your instrument.* Audio books are a tremendous resource. Many are available for free at your local public library. You can increase your knowledge while walking, driving, or doing housework.

10. *Attend band, orchestra, and professional soloist concerts.* Become inspired by attending workshops and clinics provided by the best professionals in your field. Distance learning is an increasingly available option. However, live interaction is still the best learning opportunity

for most people. There is something achieved by being in the same room with other like-minded people who are open to receiving the information and good vibes provided by an expert.

CHART YOUR PRACTICE

When students were given the "checklist for success," a practice record often was attached. If an activity is vital to achieving your goals, consider keeping a record, journal, or diary. For example, just the act of writing down what you eat increases your consciousness of nutritional intake. Maintaining a daily record of progress will keep your goals firmly in mind.

Chapter Seven

Group Interaction in Music

Our experience in band took us from a day when an obsession with individualism and cynicism was prevalent and placed us in active participation in a community that gave people, young and old, a sense of worth and meaning, that reminded us that people can make a difference, do count for something. Once again we were grabbing at sunbeams and daring to dream.

—Phil Dare, Lafayette High School Band Parent, May 1996

BAND: A GROUP OF PEOPLE UNITED IN A COMMON PURPOSE

Much can be accomplished when people work together in joy. If you begin to feel resistance, it is a warning indicator that people are working at cross purposes and not moving in the same direction. In the world of drum and bugle corps, there is a saying, "One corps, one score." It's the same group concept in band, but it doesn't rhyme as well. "One band, one aggregate assessment result" just doesn't have the same ring to it. In drum and bugle corps competitions, there are individual caption scores that reflect achievement in music performance, visual performance, and general effect. Scores are assigned to various sections of the corps, including the brass, percussion, and color guard. "One corps, one score" is derived from the idea that the only score that matters is the overall score. Focusing on individual areas can lead to competition within the group, blame, and negative energy. When you rehearse, perform, travel, eat, sleep, and live together 24/7 for months, having a cooperative spirit is vital to your success and enjoyment.

So, if any score is not as high as desired, everybody works to improve it. If the score of any section is exceptionally high, then everybody shares in the triumph.

As a music educator participating in competitive marching band, I never liked the individual awards, such as "outstanding drum major" or "outstanding soloist." I told my drum majors that their score was the high music score or, better yet, the overall band score. It is essential to work together toward a common goal of excellence. Any division can create dissonance within the group. When the entire group is responsible for all aspects of the performance, it promotes understanding, caring, and compassion for others. Any organization should decide on a common goal; believe in everyone's ability to achieve the goal; take an agreed-upon course of action toward achieving the goal; and share the credit and celebrate together when the goal is accomplished. Indeed, "one corps, one score." This is fundamental to creating cooperation—and success—within any group.

TUNE IN

When you hear an oboist play a tuning note at the beginning of a concert, the sound is vibrating at 440 cycles per second (A = 440 Hz). The other instrumentalists hear the note, then play their instruments to compare their pitch to the standard. Woodwinds and brass adjust the length of their instrument and string players adjust the tension of their strings so that everybody is on the same wavelength. Instruments that are an octave below the oboist compare their pitch, although their A is sounding at 220 Hz. The tuba and double bass (string bass) are sounding at 110 HZ and 55 Hz, respectively. A flautist goes the opposite direction and matches pitch up an octave, at 880 Hz. During this tuning process, dozens of people, playing a variety of instruments, come to agreement on a single pitch center. Playing with others in unison is one of the most difficult skills for musicians to master; every person must sound a pitch that vibrates at exactly the same wavelength. Musicians can hear a difference of even a few cents. (There are 100 cents in a semitone, the smallest interval between notes.) In order to play in tune, a musician must have a superb level of control and an acute awareness of the pitch played by the other musicians. When playing a melody, the pitch is subjective, not absolute. Playing in tune is affected by the relationship of the note to the tonal center, the temperature in the room, and the acoustic characteristics of each instrument. It isn't enough to select the correct fingering or valve combination and play the correct note. A musician must anticipate where the pitch will be and adjust to the other musicians as quickly as possible.

Harmony occurs when more than one note is played at the same time. The basic unit of harmony is the triad—three notes played simultaneously, such as C–E–G. To play a triad in tune, each note must be played in *relationship* to the others. Advanced musicians will slightly lower the third of a major triad and raise the third of a minor triad to create a chord that "rings."

Ensemble skills don't stop with playing in tune or playing in time. Musicians are constantly blending and balancing with others. In order to blend, musicians adjust their timbre (tone color) so that it pleasingly melds into the overall sound. To balance, the musicians must adjust their volume so that each note of the triad is present in the correct proportions.

In addition to playing in time, in tune, in blend, and in balance, the musicians also must match note length, style, inflection, phrasing, and feeling. It is challenging for three people to play together in a trio; imagine the difficulty of bringing together an entire orchestra! Through an intense level of skill, awareness, and cooperation, it *is* possible, and the results are extraordinary.

BREATHE AND MOVE TOGETHER

Ensembles that play with precision and artistry breathe and move together. This is readily apparent when a string quartet, woodwind quintet, or brass quintet plays. These small chamber ensembles don't use a conductor. In order to begin together and set the tempo, the leader breathes and moves in time. One may hear an audible "sniff" from the first violinist in a string quartet. When a group of players begin or release a note together, one of them breathes and visibly moves his instrument up and down an inch or two while the other players follow in synchronicity. They do this in the same time and style as the music. If the music is *staccato* (separated) they move with a quick, detached motion. If the music is *legato* (connected),

they move with a smooth, sustained motion. If the musical phrase is leading toward a goal note, or if the musicians intend for a note to have more
emphasis, they will physically lean into it. Similarly, if the music calls
for the energy to dissipate, the players will recline back. A body language
develops among players that helps achieve precision and coordinates the
musical inflections and nuances.

While all of the players are breathing and moving together, one player
is the leader and the others follow by watching the motion and listening
to the breath. The leader is not always the same person; it is determined
by who has the primary responsibility in the music. This may change
throughout a composition. A musician's title—first violin or first trumpet—seniority, or experience is irrelevant. The leader is determined ex-
clusively by the needs of the music.

IT GOES WITHOUT SAYING

Communication by body language is also important in large ensembles.
Players follow the principal player in their instrument section, and section
leaders take cues from each other. In a *tutti* (full ensemble) musical moment, all of the principal players breathe and move together. In fact, all
players in the ensemble may do it if that's what the music suggests. This
breathing and moving is done in full coordination with the conductor.
Even instruments that don't require a breath to play, such as strings and
percussion, breathe and move together. This unifies the beginning of the
sound and mitigates the various response differences among instruments.
Of course, it is natural to move with the music. The organic blending of
visual and aural, cognitive and psychomotor, aesthetic and kinesthetic is
one of the reasons a live performance is so compelling.

All of this nonverbal communication has a way of bypassing the language centers in your brain and going straight to your soul. You can literally "feel" a great concert through the seat of your pants. (Some chords
and percussion impacts actually vibrate the chairs in a concert hall.) This
is a powerful reminder that most of our day-to-day communication is
nonverbal. Humans have an incredible ability to receive the vibrations of
others through all of their senses, but perhaps most convincingly, by feeling. I believe that one of the great lessons we can learn from a musical

ensemble is that we have an impressive ability to connect, communicate, and cooperate with each other without ever saying a word.

GET IN THE FORM

There is a visual equivalent to "tuning in" in marching band. When a band creates a formation on the field, each performer is assigned an X, Y coordinate. This determines the exact location of each performer on the field in relationship to the vertical yard lines and horizontal hash marks. Each person represents one point in a linear or curvilinear formation. A person can be in the correct position on the field yet not be "tuned in" to the formation. Therefore, band members develop the skill of adjusting their position on the field in relation to the people around them so that the form looks correct to the audience. Similar to playing the correct note and then "tuning," once people have arrived at the correct location, they still need to "tune in" to the other performers.

MOVING IN RELATION TO OTHERS

Marching band shows are much more than static pictures. The formations represent perhaps only 5 percent of the show. Most of the action occurs during the transition between formations—the development of the drill. For example, a person may begin a move as part of a line with an equal spacing of 45 inches (two-step interval) between performers. During the movement, the line may morph into a curve with an interval of 67.5 inches (three-step interval). The performers must understand their relationship to the other performers as well as take the correct step size and direction of march to make the drill work correctly. Performers don't turn their heads to evaluate whether or not they are in the form as it develops; they must use their peripheral vision and any other sense that is helpful.

Keep in mind that, as a performer, movements may be executed while marching backward with the upper body turned in the direction of the audience and the instrument pointed toward the press box. Percussionists manipulate heavy, awkward equipment. Auxiliary members twirl batons (which may or may not be on fire), thrust poms or spin flags, rifles, or sabers as they dance across the field. Other sections may pass through the formation. And keep in mind that the musicians still play instruments as they move and must be aware of all previously mentioned musical relationships: playing in time, in tune, in blend, and in balance. By the way, they can't forget to watch the drum major. These movements are executed on a field outside in all kinds of weather. And, of course, all while playing their hearts out!

I've only scratched the surface in describing the simultaneous responsibilities required of each marching band musician. Again, this is achieved through a high level of skill, awareness of others, and commitment to achieving the goal with overall excellence. It is clear that this can only be achieved with cooperation and the recognition that group members are *interdependent*. There is no room for competition, jealousy, or noncooperation. If you don't work together in a marching band, you're going to get run over by the percussion section or smacked by a spinning flag pole. Similarly, in any group, cooperation among colleagues is more important than competition among individuals. You can show up to work and be in the right place but still not be a part of the group. You can be saying all the right things but not be in harmony with the other people in your office. Not only do you need skills in the workplace but also you need an acute awareness of the other people around you and a commitment to tune into their wavelengths.

TRUST YOUR NEIGHBOR

One of the Colorado State University Marching Band's traditions is affectionately called the "trombone suicide routine." The twenty-eight members of the trombone section line up toe-to-toe and commence sounding off "down, left, down, left" to determine which direction they must move first. The cymbal section starts off a catchy percussion groove, and the rest of the band members dance. On cue, the trombones begin a head-chopping motion—one person rapidly bends down at the waist while the adjacent person swings a trombone slide over his back right where his head was the count before. (A count is less than a half second.) "Head-chop" and "suicide routine" are appropriate names for this extremely physical sequence. One mistake and you will get socked in the mouth, nose, cheek, or eye. It is fascinating to watch, and the audience loves it. Trombone players take great pride in this routine, and they enjoy a well-deserved notoriety around campus. They couldn't do this routine without each player doing his or her part to perfection—and trusting that the next person will, too.

Chapter Eight

Developing Group
Identity and Loyalty

The first step in developing group identity and loyalty is attracting quality. First-class people want to belong to a first-class organization. So how to you attract the best people to your group?

EVERYONE HAS A PURPOSE

Each person should have an essential and well-defined role. People want to contribute and feel important to the group. Psychologist Abraham Maslow first proposed his hierarchy of needs theory in the paper "A Theory of Human Motivation." This hierarchy is often represented as a pyramid in which self-esteem is near the top, even above love and belonging. Self-esteem is achieved when people know that they are an essential and appreciated part of society. We all need to feel as if we are making a contribution and are valued by others.

ATTITUDE OF GRATITUDE

People feel respected when their value is recognized. An attitude of gratitude puts everyone in a more appreciative mood. It is important to show appreciation consistently and, when possible, in a tangible way. No one should go away empty-handed from the end-of-the-year awards banquet.

PERFORMANCE WEAR

Nothing establishes group identity more quickly than a classy uniform or logo apparel. Nothing destroys group identity more quickly than an embarrassing uniform or tacky casual wear. Apparel is not just functional: A great look can improve morale and create a polished, professional image. Most people care about what their peers think of them. Their public image and self-image is affected by their appearance. Therefore, one criterion for selecting a uniform is how people will feel about wearing it in front of their peers. If the apparel is also comfortable and appropriate to the function, then it's a winner.

What apparel is called makes a difference in how it is perceived. Here are a few working definitions: A *uniform* distinctively identifies a group, profession, or rank. It can have longevity and reflect tradition. A *costume* is associated with a culture, period, or dramatic purpose. It may be used in a specific role or for a special occasion. *Performance wear* allows or improves the execution of an activity or task. It may look like a uniform. *Identity apparel* is casual wear with a logo, color, or other identifying characteristic of a group. It often is called logo apparel.

CLARK KENT BECOMES SUPERMAN
BY PUTTING ON LYCRA

Once the uniform, costume, or performance wear is chosen, it is important to establish standards for its wear and care. The classiest bands are always seen in public wearing full uniform, never partial uniform. If a hat is worn, it is worn correctly, never turned backward or tilted to the side. This reinforces the image of the band as a special performing organization, instills pride in the group appearance, and enhances the public's perception of the band. My friend, Dan Berard, refers to uniforms as "Superman suits" because of their transformational power. I haven't been trained in the Walt Disney Co. philosophy, but it is common knowledge that Disney employees are called "cast members." When they are in costume, the public never sees them eat, sleep, rest, smoke, chew gum, or otherwise be out of character. I once went to a prominent chain restaurant and, dining by myself, took a seat at the bar. At the time, I was the conductor of the Central Kentucky Youth Orchestra. I wore a polo shirt with the orchestra's logo and khaki pants. I got several funny looks from the employees before I realized that my outfit was almost identical to their restaurant uniform. Employees were not allowed to sit at the bar in company attire. Come to think of it, I probably should not have been drinking a beer in public wearing my youth orchestra logo shirt. Next time, I'll bring a jacket.

WINNING THE MASTERS!

Over time, a band begins to take on the personality of its director. Sometimes, this is a good thing; sometimes, not so much. When I arrived at Colorado State University, it had not had a director of bands for fourteen years. The band's building was old and not well maintained. I sensed that an injection of pride in the organization was overdue. I started by cleaning my office, painting the walls, and buying new furniture and comfortable seating. I tried to make it look professional and welcoming. Some band members and I cleaned and organized the main rehearsal room. To brighten the room, which had a twenty-foot ceiling, I borrowed a ladder from the theater department and uncovered historic skylights that had been painted over. (Because I did this without permission, I received a reprimand letter in my file, but we enjoyed a much nicer atmosphere.)

I also bought as many suits as I could afford and I wore one every day, even though the building didn't have air-conditioning. While I was overdressed for the casual atmosphere of the West, it helped establish an image of professionalism. Some band members wrote in their evaluations that they appreciated my professional attire. Over the years, the band's self-image improved and, perhaps as a result of that, so did its public image. For marching band performances, I bought a couple of sport coats in school colors. Our colors are green and gold, so I bought a green sport jacket. At a football game, a beer-drinking fan razzed me, "Hey man, congrats on winning the Masters!" This was a not-so-flattering reference to the green jacket bestowed on the winner of the famous golf tournament in Augusta, Georgia. I don't wear that jacket anymore, but they still sell beer at the games.

YOU CAN'T PLEASE EVERYBODY

When it came time to purchase uniforms for the Colorado State band, I
hired one of the most creative and innovative designers in the country,
Michael Cesario. My enthusiasm was dampened somewhat when I began
to consider the challenges of designing a uniform. It must look good on
all body types: men and women, tall and short, athletic and not so athletic.
The person wearing it must be able to march, run, dance, play, and drum
for as long as eight hours in weather than can range from 100 degrees and
sunny to 9 degrees and snowing. Plus, the uniform must appeal to a wide
range of people, including:

1. the band members who wear it;
2. the high school students the band wants to recruit;
3. the college students who cheer on the band;
4. the university administrators who find the money to pay for the uniforms;
5. the athletic department officials responsible for the game atmosphere;
6. the general public of all ages and backgrounds.

The Colorado State uniform presents some additional challenges as
well. Green and gold are great school colors but not so good for a marching band. Too much green blends into the field during a performance.
Therefore, the uniform has a lot of a neutral color, white. But white tends
to make people look bigger. So why not black, which is slimming and
looks classy? Well, it turns out that our big rival's school colors are black
and gold, so even though our school color is gold, if we pair it with black
no one on the above list will be happy. Okay, so how about more gold?
Have your ever seen gold pants on anyone besides a Las Vegas dancing
girl? Speaking of dancing girls, we also create costumes for our dance line
(poms), color guard (flags), and drum majors (whose behinds are the primary physical attribute the audience sees). Additionally, the uniform must
make sense when we perform all types of shows: traditional marches,
rock, Latin, swing, or even Broadway musicals. So, selecting a uniform
for the Colorado State band is a big challenge.

I am personally drawn to edgy, innovative costumes. But I soon realized that our initial concept didn't provide the university identity we

wanted. When the band marches down the street in a parade or into the stadium, everyone should take notice and say, "Hey, here comes the CSU Band!" not "Hey, is there a *Star Trek* convention in town?" My creative approach did not accomplish that goal, so I shelved my personal taste and asked for a design that was fresh but respected the traditions and identity of the university. Cesario nailed it.

Everybody knows when Superman shows up, because he is wearing red, yellow, and blue spandex with a big *S* on his chest. When the Colorado State University band appears, everybody recognizes the green and gold (and white) colors and the embroidered Ram worn proudly over each member's heart.

"WHO ARE YOU?"

At the conclusion of every rehearsal, the Lafayette Band stands at attention. The director asks in cadence, "Who are you?" and the members respond, "Lafayette Band, pride of the Bluegrass, sir!" I don't know when this tradition began, but it probably was soon after the slogan was conceived in the 1960s. When I was in the band in the 1970s, we did it. As director, I used it in the 1980s and 1990s. It is a tradition to this day. I loved to change it up sometimes and ask, "Who's the best?" or after a big win, "Who's the state champ?" The band members loved it, and I admit I got chills when I heard it. Solidarity. Spirit. Belonging. Pride. Tradition.

"EAT 'EM UP"

I also like the favorite chant at Colorado State: "I'm proud to be a CSU Ram, I said I'm proud to be a CSU Ram." It has a good beat—and it's upbeat. It is much better than another favorite, "Eat 'em up, spit 'em out, Ram it up your (insert mascot here)." It's one thing to "Ram it up" the Buffaloes, but when you are playing the Aztecs. . . . It reminds me of the chant in the middle of the fight song at the University of South Carolina, where I went to school. The Carolina mascot is the "Fighting Gamecock." The march, "Step to the Rear," has two beats of silence, during which the entire crowd yells, "Go Cocks!" It still makes me chuckle.

Another well-known, yet questionable, chant comes from Sam Walton, founder of Wal-Mart. It goes like this:

> Give me a W!
> Give me an A!
> Give me an L!
> Give me a squiggly! (*shake your booty*)
> Give me an M!
> Give me an A!
> Give me an R!
> Give me a T!
> What's that spell?
> Wal-Mart!
> Whose Wal-Mart is it?
> It's my Wal-Mart!
> Who's No. 1?
> The customer, always!

It's proven to be a lot more popular in America than in other countries.

These chants tend to be cheesy unless they evolve naturally and organically from within the group. Like most things, if they are imposed, they create more resistance than camaraderie.

HAPPY BIRTHDAY

I love a tradition of singing at the end of a rehearsal or meeting. The Colorado State band ritually invites anyone having a birthday to the front of the group, where they are feted with an enthusiastic rendition of "Happy Birthday to you . . ." This song was written in 1893 by two Kentucky sisters, Mildred H. Hill and Patty Smith Hill, and it is still under copyright protection. I suppose that's why you hear some silly songs being sung by the staffs of national chain restaurants—to avoid paying royalties on "Happy Birthday." That's fine with me, because many people don't sing it well. Every time I hear the song mangled, it makes me uneasy about the state of music education in America. I'm no singer, but in the spirit of trying to improve the musical experience for everyone, here are some tips:

1. If you are leading the song, sound a starting pitch for a few seconds until everybody is humming along. It doesn't matter if it is an actual note or not. At least the group has a fighting chance of singing in tune.
2. Start the song in the lower part of your comfortable vocal range. The first note is the lowest note in the ditty. The third time you sing "happy birthday," the interval is an octave, which is a pretty big skip. If you start in the middle or upper part of your range, you may not be able to hit the high note. A lot of people don't sing the full octave, and that's when you usually hear some type of bizarre interval—or people just give up and start chanting.
3. If you want to conduct as people sing, remember the song is in 3/4 meter and it begins on beat 3.
4. If you are a musician, please note that the song begins on the fifth scale degree (*sol*) and ends on the tonic (*do*). So, if someone says, let's play "Happy Birthday" in the key of C, you should begin on G. My friend, the late composer and violinist Andreas Makris, told me that the concertmaster of the National Symphony Orchestra once made the mistake of calling the key and then beginning on the tonic instead of the dominant. He became embarrassed when bitonality (two simultaneous tonal centers) ensued.

After the band sings "Happy Birthday," we end by singing the school alma mater with our arms around each other and swaying in rhythm. It connects all sections of the band and provides a warm feeling of unity and harmony. When I first came to Colorado State, I forgot to sing the alma mater a few times. People let me know, in no uncertain terms, not to make that mistake again.

THE SUN SHINES BRIGHT

My all-time favorite song is sung at the conclusion of every University of Kentucky Marching Band rehearsal and before each performance. Director Harry Clarke started the tradition in the 1960s, and it continues to this day. The group gathers, focuses, and sings "My Old Kentucky Home," by Stephen Collins Foster. The band members actually know the lyrics, unlike the crowd at football and basketball games, who mostly chime in on the chorus, "Weep no more my lady . . ." My friend Milton Minor, a UK Band alumnus, knows all of the verses. This knowledge serves as a sort of secret musical handshake among true Kentuckians.

Legend has it that Foster wrote "My Old Kentucky Home" in the early 1850s during a visit to a cousin's plantation, Federal Hill, in Bardstown, Kentucky. The song is about slaves, whom the original lyrics referred to as "darkies." The Kentucky General Assembly officially substituted "people" for "darkies" in 1986. Still, some people refuse to sing the song because they think it has racist overtones. I respect that. The public also sings "*my* old Kentucky home" instead of "*the* old Kentucky home," which is how the song was written. This makes sense and is more personal to anyone who has ever loved Kentucky. I once had the opportunity to conduct the UK band with the venerable Happy Chandler—former governor, senator, and baseball commissioner—singing in front of twenty-four thousand people at Rupp Arena, home of the Kentucky "Wildcat" basketball team. What a moment! The song brings Kentuckians together in community, which is perfect for a state with the motto, "United We Stand, Divided We Fall." After I moved to Colorado, our team played the University of Louisville in the 2000 Liberty Bowl. During the pregame ceremonies, the U of L band played "My Old Kentucky Home." With a lump in my throat, I sang my heart out.

Here's the song's first verse, courtesy of the Kentucky Department for Libraries and Archives:

"My Old Kentucky Home"
by Stephen Foster
Original Lyrics (1853)

The sun shines bright in the old Kentucky home,
'Tis summer, the darkies are gay;
The corn-top's ripe and the meadow's in the bloom,
While the birds make music all the day.

The young folks roll on the little cabin floor,
All merry, all happy and bright;

By 'n' by Hard Times comes a-knocking at the door,
Then my old Kentucky home, goodnight.

Chorus
Weep no more my lady
Oh! weep no more today!
We will sing one song for the old Kentucky home,
For the Old Kentucky Home far away.

PURPLE MOUNTAINS

Now that I live in Colorado, I have come to fully appreciate the song "America the Beautiful." Katharine Lee Bates wrote the lyrics after a visit to Pikes Peak, near Colorado Springs. If you have ever visited the Colorado mountains, you can understand how someone could be inspired to write such beautiful poetry. Samuel A. Ward composed the music. I would prefer "America the Beautiful" as our national anthem, instead of "The Star-Spangled Banner." It is easier to sing, emphasizes peace rather than war, and lends itself to stunning instrumental arrangements.

I doubt that every organization can, or should, sing together at the conclusion of a gathering. Perhaps this should occur spontaneously, as when people first gathered after the World Trade Center attacks in New York City. I understand that they sang "Amazing Grace," "America the Beautiful," and "We Shall Overcome." The New York Philharmonic performed Brahms's *Requiem*. I think it is important to note that the first communal response to the horrific events of September 11, 2001, was singing and a concert.

I am glad to be involved in organizations whose members have enough heart and sensitivity to enjoy singing together. If the opportunity presents itself, or if there is an emotional song appropriate for your group, consider beginning a new tradition—one that unifies your people in harmony.

Chapter Nine

Competition and Cooperation within Competition

Tom and Harry, two young band directors, sat at a bar discussing the music they were playing next year. An older conductor walked in with his new, much younger wife. Tom said, "Hey, check out Dick's new trophy wife." To which Harry replied, "Yeah, I see her. Evidently, he didn't get first place."

I told a more personal version of this joke as an icebreaker to colleagues at a marching band conference. It just happened to be the day before my wedding. Nervous laughter ensued. I'm not sure if I offended the competitive band directors or the married folk. Fortunately, my wife, Kimberly, laughs loudly at this poor attempt at humor. But the discussion of competition in band never fails to elicit a passionate response in people.

While there is a lot of cooperation in music, there is also a lot of competition. Competitions often fall into one of three categories: ratings, placements, or individual awards. Marching bands usually compete for placements. A winner is chosen, and the bands are placed in rank order. Sometimes they are divided by class, which is usually determined by the size of the schools or bands.

Jazz and concert bands usually participate in festivals for ratings. Traditionally, these are:

I — Superior
II — Excellent
III — Good
IV — Fair
V — Poor

There is no set number of each rating to be awarded, so each band can receive a rating of superior, although that rarely happens.

Under the umbrella of bands, there are competitions for indoor percussion ensembles and indoor color guards, usually for placements. Band students participate in solo and ensemble festivals for ratings. Musicians often audition for placement in bands and chair position within sections. Auditions are held for leadership positions, such as section leader or drum major. Concerto competitions are popular with orchestras, where a soloist is selected to perform with the ensemble. And there is no shortage of singing competitions.

Competition is part of our culture. It is inherent in our schools, our workplaces, and our economy. Many people, though, believe that cooperation is a more appropriate paradigm for the development of organizations. Youth typically pass through three stages on the way to adulthood: dependence, independence, interdependence. Children are dependent on adults; adolescents strive for independence; and adults generally recognize that interdependence is important. Interdependence occurs when there is a natural association or an interrelationship that is mutually beneficial. Author Stephen Covey has encouraged us to look for the "win-win." We will consider cooperation and interdependence more in the next chapter. But sometimes, regardless of our feelings about competition, we become engaged in it. Participation in band provides a provocative approach to competition. In this chapter, I will discuss some strategies for dealing with competition—and some down-home Kentucky wisdom.

COMPETE WITH YOURSELF, NOT OTHERS

The Rev. Robert Schuller, in his early writings, advises us to "compete with yourself, not others." The idea is that you can never lose when you compete against yourself. Furthermore, you are not trying to beat someone else. In his book *No Contest,* Alfie Kohn writes, "The simplest way to understand why competition generally does not promote excellence is to realize that trying to do well and trying to beat others are two different things." Unlike most sports, there is no defense in band. Bands aspire to perform to the best of their ability and be happy for the other bands in the contest. Trying to be better than you were yesterday or last week or last year can be highly motivating, and it can lead to steady improvement. But there is no doubt that vying for the championship trophy can also lead to a strong effort by everyone in the group. Sometimes this is fueled by fear motivation—the fear of losing, disappointment, disgrace, or humiliation. But a healthier, more sustainable approach is to return to the CBA's of Success: Conceive It, Believe It, Achieve It.

Embrace the creative process by imagining what you or your organization wants to become. Then allow that image to be realized through your thoughts and actions. Many bands embrace this philosophy while still participating in contests. They are concerned only with that which they can control—their own preparation and performance. In other words, they bring their artistic vision to the venue, enjoy performing for the audience, and reap the rewards of their accomplishment, regardless of placement in the contest. Because they can't control what the judges think, they focus entirely on their own capabilities to express themselves artistically. They let the chips fall where they may without much regard for a subjective outcome. This uses the "cornucopia" theory—there is enough to go around for everybody. Coincidentally, bands that take this approach often win their share of trophies. Focusing on the positive aspects of excellence in performance attracts success; fixating on the negative goal of beating someone else invites failure—and unhappiness.

BEYOND FLOW

When bands perform at their highest level of artistry, without regard for extrinsic rewards, contests transcend competition. They become venues that showcase the unveiling of human potential. They become places where band members engage in an incredible spectacle that combines art and the striving for human achievement. In doing so, they establish a connection with a crowd that is supportive and appreciative. The band members experience a condition that exceeds "flow" and becomes "exhilaration." It is cooperation and interdependence at its highest level. The artistry exceeds the mundane world of numbers and rankings. This is why people who have experienced this showcase of human endeavor know in their heart that it is good. It resonates. It attracts positive feelings. It is not about beating others; it is about striving and thriving and sharing it with others. We will explore this phenomenon in more depth later.

Of course, there are some who participate in these competitions who have not yet achieved the aforementioned purity of heart. Some come with the intention of beating others. This is a zero-sum game. I have seen bands that have performed exceedingly well and yet feel excessively poor. One minute they are performing their hearts out and the next they are bawling their eyes out. On the one hand, it is an emotional reaction that shows a deep level of caring. This is positive. On the other, it entirely misses the point.

One of my fondest memories, and one of the Lafayette Band's finest moments, occurred in October 1994 at a contest in Nashville, Tennessee. We gave a well-executed and emotional performance of our *Les Misérables* show. It felt good. I was pleased. Afterward, we sat together as a group and enjoyed a performance by the McGavock High School Band, directed by Jeff Beckman and Nola Jones. This band was a perennial powerhouse, and its performance was stunning. It was warm, effervescent, and visceral. Our band members hung on every note and every flag toss. All of us recognized that we had just witnessed an amazing performance by a thoroughly committed band. We stood on our feet in appreciation. After the show, we gathered to reflect as a group. No one felt diminished by the fact that we received second place. It just opened our eyes to what we could become. We went home with higher goals. We set our sights on achieving more than we had dreamed to that point. That season culminated in some of the best-executed and most emotional performances I have ever experienced as a band director. We could thank our McGavock friends for setting the bar high, and we could feel good that our approach was based on the pure, positive intention of being our best and not on being better than someone else.

One of the problems with focusing too much on winning is that it is easy to lose sight of the fundamental goal, which in band is to create art. This is common for musicians in many areas, not just band. It can occur any time too much emphasis is placed on the quality of performance rather than the nature of the experience. Mihaly Csikszentmihalyi makes this point in his book, *Flow:*

> Parents who push their children to excel at the violin are generally not interested in whether the children are actually enjoying the playing: they want

the child to perform well enough to attract attention, to win prizes, and to end up on the stage of Carnegie Hall. By doing so, they succeed in perverting music into the opposite of what it was designed to be: they turn it into a source of psychic disorder. Parental expectations for musical behavior often create great stress, and sometimes a complete breakdown.

MUSIC FOR A LIFETIME, NOT A HALFTIME

Experiencing great stress, or having a complete breakdown, also happens to individuals in groups that rehearse too much, demand an inordinate amount of time, and overemphasize competition. Too often, students who have participated in competitive marching band put their instrument in its case after high school and never play again. They are simply burned out. The joy of music has been vanquished, and any hope of becoming a lifetime participant in music is dead. Referring to bands, which often work on their halftime shows to the detriment of real musical learning, composer Robert W. Smith coined the phrase, "Music for a lifetime, not a halftime."

DOWNWARD SPIRAL

On the other foot, high school marching bands that don't compete are often not very good. They don't achieve excellence in music performance, marching execution, or quality of show design. They rarely stay up with the latest innovations. Equipment and uniforms are generally not a priority. Because the experience is not optimal, people are not attracted to it. Because people are not attracted to it, resources are not available. Because resources are not available, people make excuses. And the worse it gets, the worse it gets. Sometimes, bands that don't compete practice as much as, or more than, competitive bands yet get a much poorer result. I have always believed that if you are going to spend the time, you might as well get the most quality out of it. My father was fond of saying, "It's not how much time you spend; it's how you spend your time."

Both of these examples represent extremes. Noncompetitive high school bands can be just as good as competitive ones, if they choose to employ the CBA's of Success: Conceive It, Believe It, Achieve It in regard to their level of achievement. There are many examples of this at the college level. And competitive bands can maintain the joy and love for making music so long as they are focused on art rather than trophies.

One of the beautiful aspects of competition is that it allows people to clarify their goals. Why do car manufacturers race? It is expensive and potentially damaging to public perception, not to mention the environment. They do it because it has long been a breeding ground for innovation. Many of these lessons from the racetrack find their way into passenger cars and commercial vehicles on the highway. We can thank the automotive engineers who develop racecar technology for many of the performance enhancements and safety systems we take for granted in our daily commute. Similarly, I can trace most of the concepts I use in developing noncompetitive college marching band shows to the highly competitive heritage of drum and bugle corps and high school marching band.

TOP TEN REASONS WHY SOMETIMES
THE BEAR GETS YOU

This is a Top 10 list of the principles that contributed to our bands' success in competition. These sayings are primarily from my father, J. Larry Moore. Even though he was well educated and well traveled, he delivered these aphorisms in the down-home vernacular of rural Kentucky. Feel free to add a dash of southern inflection as you read them. I will do my best to translate.

1. You can't win the Indy 500 in a Chevette. Translation: Develop the best product.

Chevettes were not renowned for their speed or quality; I know, because I drove one. In band, if the members don't have a good show, it doesn't matter how hard they work on it. It's important to provide your band (or sales team) with the very best product. Find or develop the best possible product. Then sell it.

2. If you can't take the heat, stay out of the kitchen. Translation: Don't enter a competition unless you are willing to accept the results.

If you are going to take credit when you win, you must be willing to accept responsibility when you lose. It is poison to complain about "getting cheated" or "the judges don't understand us" after the contest. The time to consider the quality of the process is before you enter, not after the results are announced. If you don't think it is a valid process, don't get involved.

Expect any competition to be intense. Enter a business or profession you respect and be prepared to work hard and passionately.

3. Leave no stone unturned. Translation: Be thorough in preparation.

Be passionate to the point of fanaticism. (Okay, maybe stop just short of fanaticism, but teeter near the edge.) Dedicate your life to the pursuit of the dream. Involve your family so they don't feel ignored. Every detail is critical, no matter how small or insignificant it may seem. (When the Lafayette Band slept in a gym, band members lined up their sleeping bags. "The band that sleeps in line, marches in line.") Do whatever it takes, whether or not you want to do it. Make a list of everything that you possibly can do, prioritize the list, then forget the priorities and do everything on the list.

There is no difference between band and most businesses or professions in this regard.

4. Don't leave the door open. Translation: Perfection expected; excellence tolerated.

When I complained about the results of a contest (see rule No. 2), Dad would often reply, "Well, son, you left the door open." In other words, there was an obvious flaw in the band's performance. Something was out of tune, the tone was not mature, someone was out of line, or there was a spacing error. Or maybe the show just didn't have enough passion. Dad's goal for the week before the biggest performance of the year was to make absolutely certain that nobody could see or hear a flaw in the show. Just by setting this expectation, the band usually achieved it.

Some professions do not tolerate mistakes. Airline pilots and surgeons come to mind. Perfection is the goal; excellence is tolerated.

5. Be so much better than everyone else that there is no doubt. Translation: Exceed all expectations.

Have you ever noticed that when your football team is up by only six points near the end of the game, the other team scores a touchdown and wins? Dad's solution was to be up by the band equivalent of two touchdowns. Band contests are subjective evaluations of quality. Intelligent people can disagree. Sometimes—and I am sorry to be the one to report this—a judge may not get all of the bands in the right order. Dad's goal was for his band to be so much better than the others that even the least-experienced judge could see it.

This was one of Walt Disney's philosophies. Disney rides are overengineered for safety. Every employee, even the street sweeper, is trained in exceptional customer service, and the parks are as clean today as the day they opened. The entire experience is designed to exceed expectations.

6. *You learn more from defeat than victory.* Translation: Learn from experience.

I must have learned a lot at the beginning of my career as a band director because I didn't win as many contests as I wanted to. However, the more it stung, the more I learned. With each experience, I grew in knowledge and determination. At a band contest, you receive a recording of each judge's comments during the performance. Some contests have seven or eight judges for the preliminary and the final competitions. I estimate that I listened to around five hundred recordings in ten years. But I didn't just listen; I *studied* with musical scores and drill charts as I listened. I took notes and found the patterns in their comments. I scrutinized the best bands. The first year, when we did not make the finals competition at the big show, the entire band sat in the stands and watched it all. That's the last time we had that "learning opportunity."

Most successful business people list a past failure as one of their reasons for current success. Edison is quoted as saying, "I have not failed. I have just found 10,000 ways that won't work."

7. *That's real good—good's a III.* Translation: Good is bad in comparison to excellent and superior.

Contests rank bands, and festivals rate bands. You know from earlier in this chapter that the ratings are as follows:

I — Superior
II — Excellent
III — Good
IV — Fair
V — Poor

There is nothing wrong with getting a II or a III at festival. If the band performs well and has learned a lot, then that may be the best rating possible for that group. But it is important not to be satisfied with "good" if "excellent" or "superior" is possible. If I ever said, "That sounds pretty good to me," Dad would usually reply, "Yes, that's real good." (Pause for effect.) "Good's a III." Sometimes, Dad would attend one of my band's rehearsals, and the conversation afterward would go something like this:

Dad: "My God, son, that's a III if I've ever heard one."
Me: "Seriously? I thought it was pretty good. So did the judges last week."
Dad: "Well, good's a III and those judges were too soft on you. I care enough to tell you the truth."

Translation: Roll up your sleeves and go to work. It's good; now, make it better.

The marketplace does not tolerate average. There are many examples of a product or service that was good, but the business failed because the alternatives were better.

8. *Sweet talk the competition, don't criticize; it makes 'em work harder.* Translation: Appreciate your competition in public and private.

Truthfully, it is important to appreciate others. There is never a good reason to criticize people in your profession. Embrace the idea behind Ronald Reagan's Eleventh Commandment: "Thou shalt not speak ill of any fellow Republican." Athletic coaches always compliment the opponent. Every team they play sounds unbeatable when you hear them talk. They must learn this in coaches' school. Besides, why provide your opponent with any extra motivation?

9. *Don't stop just because you come to a hurdle.* Translation: Expect challenges.

There will always be challenges, so expect them. You don't stop when you come to a hurdle in life; you go over it, through it, under it, around it, or burn it. Just don't stop.

10. *Sometimes you get the bear; sometimes the bear gets you.* Translation: You can't win them all.

After you have done your best, feel satisfied in that knowledge and enjoy life. There will be another day.

Chapter Ten

Cooperation and Interdependence

Interdependence is and ought to be as much the ideal of man as self-sufficiency. Man is a social being. Without interrelation with society he cannot realize his oneness with the universe or suppress his egotism. His social interdependence enables him to test his faith and to prove himself on the touchstone of reality.

—Mahatma Gandhi, *Young India*

In the last chapter, I started with the idea that competition is part of our culture. But so is cooperation. The ability to cooperate and work with others is an essential component of success in every workplace. In his book, *The Seven Habits of Highly Effective People,* Stephen Covey writes:

Independent thinking alone is not suited to interdependent reality. Independent people who do not have the maturity to think and act interdependently may be good individual producers, but they won't be good leaders or team players. They're not coming from the paradigm of interdependence necessary to succeed in marriage, family or organizational reality.

Furthermore, the world is becoming more interconnected. The Internet is a global communication system that connects computers, and thus, people. Wikis are now used to cocreate collaborative websites, including encyclopedias and any number of social networking tools. There are many examples of cooperation among industry, government, and consumers, even in the ultracompetitive automotive industry. When General Motors developed an improved crash test dummy, they shared it freely with government regulators and the rest of the auto industry. This sharing of technology improved the effectiveness of air-bag restraint devices and resulted in fewer auto injuries and fatalities.

Globalization has many definitions and ramifications, both positive and negative. But in its broadest sense, it occurs when the people of the world become more connected and function together in ways that used to be reserved for local or regional relationships. In his book, *The World Is Flat*, journalist Thomas Friedman explains that, for better or worse, globalization is occurring at a quickening pace and has huge implications for commerce and many other aspects of society. Even though there is still competition among nations, interdependence is the future; to ignore or resist it is to miss its potential.

World leaders regularly encourage cooperation and interdependence when discussing their vision for progress.

On May 19, 2009, United Nations Secretary-General Ban Ki-moon called for renewed commitment to the goal of nuclear disarmament. "We live in an age of interdependence . . . (where) cooperation replaces confrontation, where creativity replaces stalemate."

In a speech to the 2009 graduates of New York University, Secretary of State Hillary Clinton said, "There is no problem we face here in America or around the world that will not yield to human effort, to cooperation, to positive interdependence . . ."

On July, 7, 2009, President Barack Obama spoke to an audience at the New Economic School in Moscow about relations between the United States and Russia. He emphasized cooperation and interdependence over competition and domination:

> Like President Medvedev and myself, you're not old enough to have witnessed the darkest hours of the Cold War, when hydrogen bombs were tested in the atmosphere, and children drilled in fallout shelters, and we reached the brink of nuclear catastrophe. But you are the last generation born when the world was divided. At that time, the American and Soviet armies were still massed in Europe, trained and ready to fight. The ideological trenches of the last century were roughly in place. Competition in everything from astrophysics to athletics was treated as a zero-sum game. If one person won, then the other person had to lose. . . . given our interdependence, any world order that tries to elevate one nation or one group of people over another will inevitably fail. The pursuit of power is no longer

a zero-sum game—progress must be shared . . . when new connections are forged among people, all of us are enriched.

Perhaps the most improbable example of interdependence in recent history occurred in Iraq. War is the ultimate zero-sum game—win or lose, live or die. Or is it? Former Secretary of State Colin Powell warned of the "Pottery Barn rule"—if you break it, you own it. (By the way, Pottery Barn says it doesn't have such a rule, although many other stores do.) Our initial success, touted as "Mission Accomplished," quickly disintegrated into a quagmire of senseless death and destruction. But even in this theater of conflict-without-end, the most successful military tactic has been dubbed "winning hearts and minds." Our greatest modern military hero, General David Petraeus, demonstrated that you cannot bomb your way to peace and that "shock and awe" does not result in freedom and democracy. But you *can* achieve relative peace and harmony through cooperation, understanding, and relationship building. Imagine— conciliation through cooperation, not domination. Our most enlightened military leadership advocating cooperation and communion as a means to a sustainable civilization. No wonder they produce some of the world's greatest bands.

RALPHIE THE BUFFALO AND CAM THE RAM TAKE THE FIELD

In the foreword to Patrick Henry Hughes's book, *I Am Potential,* Bryant Stamford relates the power of Patrick and the University of Louisville Marching Band to calm thousands of rowdy fans. This reminded me of a similar experience I had between rival schools, Colorado State University and the University of Colorado. The annual Rocky Mountain Showdown has become quite a spectacle, in both the positive and negative sense of the word. It is a great day for football fans and attracts seventy-thousand-plus to Mile High Stadium. It also seems to encourage vitriolic behavior among otherwise normal people. One year, forty drunken fans "barricaded" the Colorado State band, launching beer and glass bottles into the band and physically assaulting band members and staff. In this case, solidarity and sobriety prevailed; the band marched in formation through the miniriot without reacting to the attacks. Inside the stadium, tens of thousands of "fans" (in this case true to the root word, *fanatic*) chanted obscenities and booed anything that represented the opposing team.

But a strange thing happened when bands from both schools took the field simultaneously. Even the crowd's biggest jerks realized they couldn't boo the opposing school without also booing their own. Earlier in the day, the University of Colorado band, under the direction of Matthew Roeder and Allan McMurray, extended hospitality to the Colorado State band by providing a rehearsal facility and a welcoming atmosphere. The two bands gathered for rehearsal and lunch. They worked together to create harmony—literally. So, when both bands (450 musicians in all) came together to perform "America the Beautiful" and "The Star-Spangled Banner," spectators ignored their team loyalties and celebrated what they had in common as sports fans, Coloradans, and Americans. Then the bands exited the field, the live ram and buffalo mascots trampled the turf, and men in battle gear bashed each other into oblivion. I don't remember who won.

CROWN THY GOOD WITH BROTHERHOOD

Bands don't get much television time any more unless they have painted faces and wear ridiculous wigs. But right after the attacks of September 11, 2001, the Colorado State band received four minutes of airtime on ABC. The football game was one of the first telecast after terrorists flew planes into New York City, Washington, D.C., and rural Pennsylvania. For months we had planned a special collaboration between our choirs and the marching band. We invited the university choir, alumni choir members, and alumni band members to join with the university marching band in a pregame performance. It was a time when the entire nation was trying to regain its sense of balance. Even a sports telecast turned to music. For a few minutes, all eyes, ears, and hearts were focused on our musicians, who resonated with the hopes and dreams of a nation in this most gracious hymn of thanksgiving, "America the Beautiful."

"America the Beautiful"
lyrics by Katharine Lee Bates

O beautiful, for spacious skies,
For amber waves of grain,
For purple mountain majesties
Above the fruited plain!
America! America! God shed His grace on thee,
And crown thy good with brotherhood,
          from sea to shining sea.

O beautiful, for pilgrim feet
Whose stern, impassioned stress
A thoroughfare for freedom beat
Across the wilderness!
America! America! God mend thine ev'ry flaw;
Confirm thy soul in self-control,
          thy liberty in law!

O beautiful, for heroes proved
In liberating strife,
Who more than self their country loved
And mercy more than life!
America! America! May God thy gold refine,
Till all success be nobleness,
          and ev'ry gain divine!

O beautiful, for patriot dream
That sees beyond the years,
Thine alabaster cities gleam
Undimmed by human tears!
America! America! God shed His grace on thee,
And crown thy good with brotherhood,
          from sea to shining sea!

NETWORK OF MUTUALITY

In previous chapters, I discussed how bands promote cooperation through all of the methods they use to play together, march together, and work together. I discussed the cooperative structures and service leadership paradigms that the best bands embrace. And I shared the exhilaration enjoyed when a group achieves more than individuals, working independently or in competition, ever could.

In the workplace, people sometimes confuse the meaning of the word *cooperation* with the willingness of one person to go along with the desires of another. True cooperation requires the agreement of people to work together for the common good. When you cooperate, you maximize productivity. Cooperation can increase enjoyment, fun, and engagement. It reduces the poisonous environment and destruction of relationships that competition can encourage. It deepens the meaning of social interaction when people recognize their interdependence. Alfie Kohn writes:

> One of the most powerful motivators is not money or victory but a sense of accountability to other people. This is precisely what cooperation establishes: the knowledge that others are depending on you. The only stake others have in your performance under a competitive arrangement is a desire to see you fail. . . . Interaction and cooperation seems to enhance each other's abilities. The group is greater than the sum of its parts.

It's true in band, it's true in the workplace, and it's true in most other aspects of life. When people work for each other, the importance of extrinsic rewards is diminished. Furthermore, when people work together for a common purpose, the ability to dream bigger and reach further is realized with tremendous power. What's more, people care about each other, and people find value in ways that affect them on a deeply personal level. This is a human experience that cements relationships with a bond that lasts well beyond the end of a project or the delivery of a paycheck.

> Moreover, I am cognizant of the interrelatedness of all communities and states. I cannot sit idly by in Atlanta and not be concerned about what happens in Birmingham. Injustice anywhere is a threat to justice everywhere. We are caught in an inescapable network of mutuality, tied in a single gar-

ment of destiny. Whatever affects one directly, affects all indirectly. Never again can we afford to live with the narrow, provincial "outside agitator" idea. Anyone who lives inside the United States can never be considered an outsider anywhere within its bounds.

—Rev. Martin Luther King Jr., "Letter from Birmingham Jail,"
April 16, 1963

Chapter Eleven

Passion in Performance, Work, and Life

Clarity of mind means clarity of passion, too; that is why a great and clear mind loves ardently and sees distinctly what he loves.

—Blaise Pascal

PLAYING WITH FIRE

If you played in my father's band, you played with fire. I'm not referring to "taking a risk," but rather "fire in the belly." There is a saying among education experts: "Teach, don't preach." Fortunately, my father didn't pay much attention to that. As a boy, when he wasn't working on the family farm, he played piano at church revivals around Gravel Switch and Lebanon, Kentucky. Fire and brimstone were part and parcel of every service. To this day, he loves any kind of music that evokes a passionate response in the musicians and the audience.

While I appreciate intellectual compositions, I like to think that I inherited some of his feeling for emotionally compelling music. I can relate to this line in Dan Fogelberg's ballad, "Leader of the Band": "But his blood runs through my instrument and his song is in my soul."

I have come to realize that this is not just a hereditary trait because many members of Dad's bands have expressed the same feelings. I believe that this is a common experience in bands, choirs, and orchestras. One of my friends remembers her experience fondly: "We may not have been the best band ever, but we put our heart and soul into it."

This doesn't just apply to music but to many other aspects of work and life. When someone gives their heart and soul, they are sharing the very core of their being. These are the kinds of people who inspire me and that I want to surround myself with. If it's worth doing well, it's worth doing with *passion*.

Passion has all the power of a Rocky Mountain river rushing relentlessly toward its destination. It cuts canyons out of granite. Its kinetic energy can nourish and power an entire region. Like a mountain stream, passion is continually in motion, never stagnant. It has the potential to create an avenue through a previously impenetrable mass. This is the type of indefatigable energy and inertia-bursting power that we all need to realize our greatest dreams.

When people are passionately inspired, they seem to have unlimited energy. They often describe the feeling as being connected with their inner spirit and or even the universal source of energy. To be inspired is to be "in the spirit," to "breathe in," to be "animated with life." The following stories help illustrate how passion can transform the mundane into the exceptional.

ONE NIGHT IN BIRMINGHAM

It was a muggy August night in Birmingham when the Spirit of Atlanta drum and bugle corps took the field for a finals performance. Marching into the stadium, corps members whistled their southern anthem in unison and moved together as a unit—physically and spiritually. The warm-up chorale, "Salvation Is Created," deepened the connection and sealed the emotional bond between performers and audience. By virtue of location, the congregation included more southerners by birth than usual. But tonight, with Spirit in the house, everyone was temporarily bestowed the title "southerner by the grace of God." All of the classics were on the program and arranged in a way that would save even the most fervent nonbeliever: "Georgia on My Mind," "Ol' Man River," "Devil Went Down to Georgia," "Sweet Georgia Brown," and "Let It Be Me." Under the lights and tapping into a higher power, the colorful guard shined like heaven's stars, the horn line sang with angelic voices, and the drum line played as if its members had made a deal with the devil himself. The emotional ballad, "Let It Be Me," was never played with more heartfelt meaning.

It was a helluva show and a helluva performance. Earlier in the summer of 1980, corps members had lost their spiritual leader and beloved drum corps idol, Jim Ott. The horn players worshipped Jim, and this was their benediction. But on that night, under the Southern Cross, twenty thousand people believed as one, and southern pride—and Jim—lived through the breath of the 128 members of the corps called *Spirit.*

As a junior staff member for the corps that summer, I met some of the finest people I've ever known. I'm thankful to have been a part of something far bigger than me. It was emotional, and, twenty-nine years later, I watched a video of the performance for the first time. Mercy!

THE PIPES ARE CALLING

Bands often achieve a level of excellence that is remarkable. Some bands transcend the remarkable and create the truly extraordinary. This occurs only when passion is an ingredient in the recipe. In an attempt to relate the experience of participating in such an organization, the following describes the action and how I felt performing in the 1976 Lafayette Band show's closing song, "Danny Boy":

The Drill

Every four counts another person arrives in a human wall forming on the 30-yard lines. The forms are consistently building along with the anticipation. As the musical phrase ends, they are complete, and the band plays the pickup notes to the piece's climax. The forms begin to rotate with total precision. The players are shoulder-to-shoulder in two lines. The color guard is in a half-circle, connecting the endpoints of the line. Its members unveil their hidden flags to create double rainbow flags, and the arcs become a solid wash of color. The flag girls carve their poles through the air, figuratively pulling the arcs around and enhancing the rotation of the form. The rifles move toward the audience on the 50-yard line with machinelike precision, then fan out into a horizontal line.

The Music

The drum line forms a nucleus of energy in the center of the field as the two giant, human pinwheels turn toward each other. As the musical line of "Danny Boy" crescendos, it builds to a climax. Both forms complete their rotation and combine in one impressive company front of musicians. The music soars as if it catches the wind and sails into the stands. It is fueled by driving percussion and the human energy of hundreds of lungs breathing in all the air they can hold and using it to generate sonic energy.

The Percussion

Drumsticks create a sustained sound through the rapid succession of strokes on the drum head. They tap with just enough force to initiate the vibration of the head and follow with the perfect bounce. The sticks rebound off the head quickly to allow it to vibrate, then return to the head to continue the roll. The low vibrations of the bass drum and timpani resonate through every person on the field and into the stands like a mild, pleasant form of electricity.

The Auxiliaries

The flag and rifle corps members stretch their spines, never taking their eyes off the audience, as they sculpt the air with their wood, aluminum, and fabric. They put their entire physical beings into the performance. The drum major feels the energy and encourages the musicians to give more and more.

The Passion

Passion is the fuel, but reason and training keep it in check. Everyone is trained to maintain control and not overblow or overhype in a way that would take away from the beauty. The entire human organism is vibrating with energy and sound. Visual. Physical. Emotional. You can smell the grass and the air that people around you exert. You taste the wooden reed or the slight bitterness of the mouthpiece on your lips. Your tongue is articulating every note as though singing a foreign language. A heartsong transcends your vocal chords as your entire being and the energy of your fellow bandsmen combine into one unified expression of desire and declaration. As the wall of musicians moves toward the audience, almost every person is playing through tears. You can't stop the emotion, but you never let it get in the way of your performance.

The Connection

Love, confidence, and pride are expressed through a complex statement of visual, musical, and physical vibrations felt by every person in the audience. Energy vibrates the air, is received by the eyes and ears, is transmitted straight down the spine, and radiates to every part of the body. As thrill bumps bubble to the surface of the skin, the energy is fed back to the performers on the field. The spectators roar.

The Final Statement

The phrase ends, and your feet begin to glide in double time with the music. The coda is frenetic with rhythm and dissonance, once again building intensity. The drum line enhances and drives the horn line. The color guard, through equipment and dance, reacts to, anticipates, and represents every rhythmic motif and nuance in the music. The forms swirl, create visual dissonance, quickly modulate, pass through each other in patterns that shouldn't even be possible, and ask physical demands of you that a few months ago were beyond your ability. But now you march it and play it and feel it as though it is an old friend.

The Release

The tension builds one last time and resolves in a final chord. It rings through the air, through your body, and through the audience. The drum major gives the final release, the sound lofts into the night air, and you hear the reverberation even as you pant for oxygen. The crowd erupts. You now understand the meaning of "reach down, give everything you have" and "play your heart out." You are exhausted, as though you just laid everything you are out on the field and there is nothing left to give.

The Audience

The energy feeds back in a cycle that is fueled by adoring, appreciative people, many of whom are parents of the band members. With lumps in their throats, they are caught up in the emotion of the music as well as pride in their children's accomplishment. The entire stadium exudes positive energy.

The Afterglow

Your performer's discipline kicks in. You keep your head up and your spine stretched. You march out in formation. Your muscle memory takes over as your conscious mind fogs, but you trust your training while you move as a unit off the field. You maintain the integrity of the group until you have exited the stadium and you are outside in the shadows of the stadium lights. You break ranks to gather with your friends, band director, staff members, and parents. It's a euphoric feeling, and everyone around you has shared it. You want to talk about it, but there are no words—none needed, just hugs. You embrace as the old and young and tall and short and black and white and brown come together in shared experience. Everyone has ridden the wave together; none could have done it without every one of the others. For a few minutes you linger in the deliciousness of the moment.

The Understanding

There is no trophy, money, publicity, or accolade that can top the experience you just had with your friends. Sensing it will never be repeated— and never forgotten—you know why band members are so passionate about what they do. They have tasted exaltation, and they will never be the same.

DOMAIN OF THE DIVINE

Earlier in this chapter, we discussed the association between living with passion and connecting with the universal source of energy and spirit. Music seems to be one of the most active channels between the mundane and the spiritual, man and God. I had an interaction with composer David Maslanka that exemplifies this relationship.

So, Are You a Couple?

David Maslanka sat across the table from us. We were waiting for chocolate soufflé. Maslanka is a composer of international renown, especially in the world of wind and percussion music. This was the first time I had met him, although I had heard his music many times and conducted one of his symphonies. I asked my new girlfriend, Kimberly, to come along, even though we had only been on a couple of dates. I knew from Maslanka's music that he had a Christian background and from my colleagues that he had an interest in Buddhism, past lives, and lucid dreaming. He confirmed that all of these had influenced the process by which he composes music.

David has an intensity about him that I attribute to his complete sincerity. He is calm when he looks at you, or rather, looks *into* you. The river of his personality runs deep, yet steady enough to allow you to see your reflection. After dessert, he asked, "So, are you a couple?" In the mirror of his inquiry, we glanced at each other, and a glimmer of recognition appeared. The glimmer soon became a beam, and our son, Jameson David Moore, became the light of our lives when he was born a year later. Two years after that, we were blessed with a bundle of radiant joy, our daughter, Lorian Sena Moore.

Ten days after Jameson was born, he went to his first concert. My parents also attended. The concert concluded with Maslanka's Symphony No. 7. The powerful, forty-minute work guided the audience through an array of human experience. It began with a reminiscence of an old-time revival piano, like my father played for churches in rural Kentucky. It continued with a nostalgically poignant flute solo. My mother played flute in the band. It concluded with a euphonium soliloquy fading into the recesses of our collective memory. My father played euphonium in the Western Kentucky University band, where my parents met. Perhaps, by coincidence, the symphony traced an arc that was congruent with the story of my family.

Maslanka's music is a direct reflection of his sincerity and authenticity in living. His long melodies spin out unhurried until they are complete. His music can be as clear as glass or as jagged as the charred fragments of

New York's World Trade Center. (He composed a response to the terrorist attacks in his work, *Testament: A Time of Trial.*) He composes as though he has a direct connection to the universal source of energy. I sense that musicians commit to his music in a manner I have rarely known. I believe that through the complete immersion of the musicians in this music, his thoughts and dreams are revealed. The universality of his understanding becomes clear to those who play his music, especially if they come to it with an open heart. Whatever you call this connection—Holy Spirit, God-force, Chi, or Kundalini—Maslanka's music is a conduit for the musicians and the audience to enter the domain of the divine.

Can't Conduct Electricity

Conductors sometimes employ self-deprecating humor by saying, "I can't conduct electricity." It's a play on words that has a particle of truth in it. In the traditional sense, a conductor leads a musical ensemble by using a baton, hands, and physical gestures. But a conductor is also that which easily transmits heat, electricity, or sound. The night I conducted Maslanka's Symphony No. 7, I was both. Through some intangible connection with the music, the band, the audience, and my family (I think of all in the hall as my *family*), every molecule was set in motion with an awe-inspiring intensity. Anyone who could not feel the energy in the room needed to have his pulse checked.

Inspiration

Throughout history, composers from Bach to the Beatles have said God (or some other label for the universal spirit) has flowed through them and manifested itself as a composition. Composers and critics agree that there is a level of craftsmanship that each composer must attain. Yet, composers have said many of their greatest works have emanated from a supernatural force; they were merely the transcriber. I have felt this union when creating the visual designs for a marching band. (Marching band drill design has evolved into a moving, visual art form.) During the creative process, the designs and motions have often come to me effortlessly. The result is a drill that meshes with the music as though it enjoys the same mathematical and spatial relationships as the harmony of the spheres. Imagining the designs, I experience "flow" and become a "flow-er" of inspired creativity. I believe that the greatest human achievements transcend flow in the creative process and connect with the passionate, inspired energy of our world.

LIVING ARTFULLY

In truth, this is what I live for. I must regularly experience moments like the one that occurred in the concert featuring David Maslanka's music. I don't want to live any other way. You can't buy this with money or recognize it with fame. It is a feeling known only to those who play music in live performance or participate in a similar shared experience. I believe that having an aesthetic experience with my group brings us closer to an understanding of art, life, and each other. When I am involved with something separate from music, I try to approach it in the same manner. I believe it is possible to create a spreadsheet that is like a work of art, design a report with all of the best intentions, or organize a project in such a way that everyone involved is changed for the better.

I don't think you need music to make these connections, although it helps. You just need people with the vision, conviction, and drive to make it all happen with excellence and passion. Do everything with love. In the University of Louisville Marching Band, Patrick Hughes's wheelchair may be pushed by his father, but his father is powered by a parent's love.

ART IS BORN

When creativity, conviction, and execution are infused with passion, art is born. Art occurs when something takes on more significance than is necessary for basic function. Art transcends the ordinary. When we create our dreams, strongly believe in them, follow a path that will lead to their realization, and pour ourselves into it with all of our heart, the result will be exceptional.

Life as inspired art—why live any other way? The alternative to passion is apathy—literally a lack of caring, emotion, or feeling. To be apathetic is to be unable to have passion. "Time-clock" employees often embody this attitude. They punch in when they begin work and punch out when the clock strikes the appointed hour. These people take little interest in the outcome of their day's work. In music, this is the equivalent of a person who only plays the notes on the page, devoid of expression, and without the ability to bring the music to life. A true artist is able to create a three-dimensional landscape that transcends an ordinary interpretation and visits the "land beyond the notes."

UNDERSTANDING TO APPRECIATION
TO LOVE TO PASSION

Passion is closely related to understanding, appreciation, and love. Understanding is achieved through education and the acquisition of knowledge. Appreciation is born out of understanding. And love is the heartfelt expression of appreciation. When you live your life with passion, you embody understanding, appreciation, and love.

And now we have come full circle to the concepts outlined at the conclusion of chapter 2: The Creative Process, but elevated in expectation: *Create, believe, and achieve with passion, while connecting with the life force inside all of us.*

Chapter Twelve

Putting It Together

LIFE IS NOT A DRESS REHEARSAL

How do you put together the concert that is your life? Is there more to it than the bumper sticker philosophy, "Life is not a dress rehearsal?" The following is an overview of the principles discussed in this book. As a summation, it necessarily moves along at a brisk tempo; I'm going to place it at *allegretto* (moderately fast). Each sentence expresses a concept that was presented in a paragraph, section, or chapter of this book. You may choose to read at a pace closer to *andante* (walking speed) in order to fully consider these concepts and how they apply to your life.

WHAT DO YOU WANT?

Life-as-art starts with the thought of what you want. The vibration of this creative thought is amplified through belief. The belief becomes expectation endowed with the strength of action. Ideas become entities. As an idea comes to mind and the desire is born and found to be good, the process by which the goal can be achieved is also conceived. By following your bliss, the process and the product are labors of love. They are joyful to do just for the pure pleasure of doing them. And when they are worth doing, they are worth doing well. Excellence becomes so ingrained that it permeates every aspect of the creation, from the initial concept through development and on to the end result.

PEOPLE ARE PARAMOUNT

The dream is so powerful that it attracts people to it. In pursuit of the dream, care and compassion for people are the priority. The well-being of everyone involved is paramount. The way you do things is always as important as the things you do. Because the leaders of any endeavor are cocreators, everyone is involved in bringing the concepts to life. The leaders serve others in such a way that everyone is valued and all reap the benefits of shared vision. As a result, each person becomes highly committed to the process and product. The commitment is shown through engagement, dedication, and enthusiasm for the task. The group begins to develop a synergy that brings about more potential than could possibly exist with people working independently. A sense of pride and loyalty to the core principles develops. People identify with the organization because they share in the mission, and the culture of the group pleases them. The group identity may be expressed through words, song, or apparel — but always through action.

HARMONY THROUGH COOPERATION

If competition is inevitable, people can rise above the trappings of extrinsic rewards and focus on staying true to their central vision and the processes they have all agreed upon. Cooperation is developed into an art. People breathe together and deliberately create harmony with others. They know their individual role, and they adjust to changing needs. Sometimes they take the lead; sometimes they support the leader. Problems are expected, but they aren't allowed to become stopping points. Every challenge is seen as a gift. The level of cooperation creates interdependence among people and ideas.

SPIRAL OF EXCELLENCE

If it's worth doing well, it's worth doing with passion. Through passion, the goals, process, and people are inspired, opening a conduit to the universal source of spirit. The connection with joy and love imbues some of the experiences to a level of transcendence. People are uplifted and inspired with work as well as the joy of being part of something greater than themselves. With each cycle, the spiral of excellence continues. As a result of past achievements, more is possible. Because people have climbed to greater heights, they can see further and envision more. Additional resources are attracted through a legacy of past success and the potential for future achievement. The exceptional becomes expected. The best becomes possible, and new benchmarks are imagined. Through this association, individuals begin to realize their own potential.

When the members of the group are high-performing, self-actualized people, the group's level of achievement surpasses expectations. The process continues and, as the saying goes, *the better it gets, the better it gets.*

ASTOUNDING POTENTIAL

I'm fortunate to often be able to work with bands other than my own. I appreciate the opportunity, and I always learn something from the experience. During these sessions, most of the time is spent making music, but we also find time to talk about the band members' individual lives in music and their aspirations for the band. I typically act out some of the leadership stories shared in this book. If the band is receptive, I tell them with all sincerity that they can be any kind of musician they want to be and that they can have any kind of band they want to have. Often, these comments are met with surprise because many people see their limitations more readily than they see their opportunities. As a visitor, it is easier for me to see their potential. Almost all bands are filled with intelligent, talented, enthusiastic people. More often than not, the leaders are well-educated, musical, and caring professionals. When you look at all of the possibilities, the potential is often astounding.

AMAZING GRACE

Our Louisville trumpeter, Patrick Hughes, couldn't imagine it any other way. In his book, *I Am Potential,* Patrick explains that being blind since birth can actually be an advantage in life. Because he doesn't see race, color, clothing, or other physical attributes, he is free to embrace each person without prejudice. He and his parents choose to make the most out of life's blessings.

I believe that all of us have the same ability as Patrick Hughes to create the life we want. And, like our beloved bands, we have the intelligence, talent, and enthusiasm to be anything we want to be. I referred to Patrick at the beginning of this book by saying, "I know this kid!" The truth is, we are *all* this kid inside. We may not have been born with the perceived *disabilities* Patrick lives with, but we have been blessed with all the *abilities* he so courageously demonstrates. We love and are inspired by people like Patrick because, at our most basic level, we believe in the boundless spirit in all of us to live and love with all of our hearts. Patrick writes that he loves being in the University of Louisville band because he is part of something larger than himself that allows him to "play his heart out." God knows, he has a big heart. And so do the rest of us. There is no limit to the dreams we can achieve, the joy we can experience, if we approach life with the heartfelt attitude of a bandsman like Patrick Hughes.

One of our most poignant transcriptions for band is a work by Morten Lauridsen. The composer sets to music the sacred text, O Magnum Mysterium, which means, "O Great Mystery." Part of the wonderment of our life's journey is examining that which we don't fully understand. I am happy for folks who think they have all of life's answers. But for those of us who don't, it is even more important that we approach living with an open heart and strengthened by the courage of our convictions.

Another classic in the band repertoire is a Russian chorale, "Salvation Is Created." The piece never fails to inspire expressive music making in choirs and bands that immerse themselves in its beauty. The English translation of the text is, "Salvation is created in the midst of the Earth, O God, Alleluia." I will let others judge the text's theological implications, but I can relate to the idea that salvation doesn't just happen, it is *created*.

Dear Dr. Moore,

This is Michael Stone from music camp. If you don't remember me, I was the trumpet player you said sounded "like butter." I just wanted to let you know that the past weeks have really taught me a lot of things. I've known ever since the eighth grade that I wanted to be a band director, but I have never felt so passionately about it as I do now. When we warmed up with *O Magnum Mysterium* Friday night before the concert, I knew then that it was going to be a great night. And when we played *Salvation Is Created*, I was so into the song emotionally that I have a new standard for my playing abilities. I now not only strive for greatness, but that amazing feeling that runs through you like new life.

Sincerely,
Michael Stone
June 2009

HOW SWEET THE SOUND

Our sweet-sounding trumpeter, Michael Stone, describes being completely immersed in the moment as "the amazing feeling that runs through you like new life." I don't think I can improve upon that description. We often hear that at the end of life, no one says, "I wish I had worked more." It has become fashionable for professors to be asked to give a talk as if it were their last lecture. While I am not quite ready to provide any end-of-life wisdom, I will say that after the final concert, I don't think anyone wants it to be said, "Nice concert. He really played that one *safe!*"

Instead, when the last release is given and the final chord rings eternal, I'd rather hear, "Amazing performance! He may have missed a few notes along the way, but Lord, *he played it from the heart!*"

Postlude: Beyond the Notes

- Look for the abilities in people, not the disabilities.
- See the similarities in people, not the differences.
- A band is a group of people united for a common purpose.
- Dream big. Dream farther than you can see. Dream it the way you want it.
- Expect the best, and you will get it.
- Set visual reminders of your goals.
- Visualize everything going perfectly.
- Look for inspiration outside of your profession.
- Believe it before you see it.
- Act as though you have already achieved your goal.
- Believe in yourself and in your unlimited potential.
- Set a plan for achieving your goals that guarantees your success.
- Do what you love, and you will never work a day in your life.
- Enjoy the process as well as the product.
- Create a template of excellence in your mind.
- Practice the way you perform, and perform the way you practice.
- Attract excellence; don't force compliance.
- If you really care about people, prepare well, follow-through, do what you say you will do, in truth and with a smile.
- Actions should embody axioms. Actions reflect values. It's not what you say, it's what you do.
- Learn each person's name; it is the most important word in his or her vocabulary.
- Praise publicly, criticize privately.
- Consider compassion instead of correction.
- It's not the years, it's the smiles.

- The better you are for others, the better it becomes for you.
- The definition of success is the ability to meet deadlines.
- If it's worth doing, it's worth doing well.
- If it's worth doing well, it's worth doing with passion.
- It's not how much time you spend; it's how you spend your time.
- Bar by bar you can be a star.
- To be early is to be on time; to be on time is to be late; to be late is to be left.
- To share in the rewards, share in the responsibility.
- Develop an attitude of gratitude.
- Look for the positive intentions behind the actions.
- Transcend competition by staying true to your core principles of excellence and artistry without regard to extrinsic rewards.
- Cooperation maximizes joy and productivity.
- When creativity, conviction, and execution are infused with passion, art is born.
- Don't play it safe; play it from the heart.

Appendix: Reflections from a Band Member

Like many high school students, my teen years were tumultuous as I struggled to find my voice, my direction in life, my purpose, and myself in the noise of adolescence. The Lafayette High School Band, under the direction of J. Larry Moore, provided a much-needed compass for me: structure, direction, and purpose. I learned so much from our director, our flag and rifle instructors, Milton Minor and Mike Williams, and my fellow travelers during that magical time, my band colleagues. I did not appreciate most of this then, but over time the kindnesses, the wisdom, the creativity, and the love has returned to me as clearly as if it had taken place last month instead of thirty years ago.

After high school, I enlisted in the U.S. Navy and spent the next six years on active duty. During those years, I found myself returning many times to lessons from band. Being in the military, and being quite young (chronologically as well as emotionally), the lesson of discipline served me well. In the military and especially in basic training, personnel are required to stand at attention for long periods of time. A thousand miles from home, wondering if I had made the mistake of my life, standing at attention felt like a little piece of home because of the rigor of the discipline we learned in band.

Years after my military experience, lessons from band returned in my professional life. Admonitions that we were "on" from the moment we stepped off the bus served me well in corporate interviews, public presentations, and other venues. I was thankful to be aware of the concept and noticed how often others were not. I have carried these lessons of friendship, respect, and determination in my heart through years in the military, as a wife and mother, an analyst, a community college dean, and now a university professor. They remain relevant and live on in stories I share with my children, students, and colleagues. The legacy of the Lafayette Band is inextricably woven into small pieces of wisdom passed on in teaching moments and shared memories all across this country, and beyond.

It mattered less that our history was that of a championship band; what mattered was that we were a group of young people who cared passionately about a single goal: achieving excellence as a unit. No textbook lesson, no lecture, no made-for-TV series can replace the learning that occurred in those band years. We lived the lessons of camaraderie, teamwork, leadership, practice, winning, losing, presentation, posture, discipline, responsibility, accountability, and respect for the process of hard work that resulted in the culmination of excellence. As I recently watched shows from 1978 and 1979, I knew that every success in my life was linked in some small way to those experiences where a bunch of kids poured everything they had into achieving something greater than themselves.

At least once in your life, it's important to be a part of something that is bigger than the sum of its parts. The band was such an entity. The experience—those years of love and loss, joy and pain—played a critical role in the development of my perspective on our place in the universe: to understand that there are things in life that are bigger than we are and that require the collective will of a number of people to be successful. This is crucial to understanding life—that we are all dependent on each other; that individual success is sweet, but that greatness is achieved most often by standing on the shoulders of the many who came before you, holding the hands of others who stand beside you.

Rebecca Harmon
Lafayette High School Band Member
Rifle Corps, 1978, 1979
Faculty, University of Pittsburgh, Pittsburgh, PA

Index

Alphin, Rich, 50–51
autotelic, 20

Beaumont Middle School, 48
Beckman, Jeff, 84
Berard, Dan, 72
beyond the notes, 108, 115–16
books and publications: "A
  Theory of Human Motivation"
  (by Abraham Maslow), 71;
  Creative Visualization (by Shakti
  Gawain), 13; *Flow* (by Mihaly
  Csikszentmihalyi), 83–85; 106–7
  (*see also* Csikszentmihalyi,
  Mihaly); *Frames of Mind* (by
  Howard Gardner), 56; *I Am
  Potential* (by P. H. Hughes and
  P. J. Hughes), 3, 37, 93, 111–12;
  Instant Replay (by Jerry Kramer),
  18; "Letter from Birmingham
  Jail" (by Rev. Martin Luther King,
  Jr.), 96–97; *No Contest* (by Alfie
  Kohn), 82, 96; *The One Minute
  Manager* (by Kenneth Blanchard
  and Spencer Johnson), 35; *Power
  versus Force* (by David Hawkins),
  28; *Psycho-Cybernetics* (by
  Maxwell Maltz), 13; *The Seven
  Habits of Highly Effective People*
  (by Stephen Covey), 91 (*see also*
  Covey, Stephen; *The World Is
  Flat* (by Thomas Friedman), 92;
  *You Can't Afford the Luxury of
  a Negative Thought* (by Peter
  McWilliams), 17; *Young India* (by
  Mahatma Gandhi), 91
Brady, Elizabeth. *See* Witherspoon,
  Elizabeth
Bratt, Doug, 39
Byrne, Gregory, 2–3, 37

Cary, Tricia, 59
Central Kentucky Youth Orchestra,
  39, 72–73
Cesario, Michael, 74–75
Chandler, Happy, 78
Chicago Symphony Orchestra, 26
Christiana High School; marching
  band, 40
Clarke, Harry, 32, 77
Clinton, Hillary, 92
Colorado State University, 1, 21,
  32–33, 56–57, 73–75, 93; marching
  band, 31, 68–69, 76–79, 93–94 (*see
  also* "trombone suicide" routine);
  wind ensemble, 9

Contest of Champions, 16, 23, 25, 49–51
cooperation, 6–8, 22, 29, 59, 63–65, 67–68, 81, 91–97, 110, 116–18
Copenhaver, James, 23
Cornish, Craig, 40, 46
Covey, Stephen, 82. *See also* books: *The Seven Habits of Highly Effective People* (by Stephen Covey)
Cramer, Ray, 22
Csikszentmihalyi, Mihaly, 19; flow, 83–84. *See also*, books: *Flow* (by Mihaly Csikszentmihalyi)
Curry, Bill, 18

Dare, Phil, 63
Deming, W. Edwards, 46
Dennison, Alyssa, 35
Devary, Alethea, 38–39
DiMartino, Vince, 53, 56
Disney, Walt, 88
drum major, 8, 12, 34, 39–40, 46, 64, 68, 74, 82, 103

Edison, Thomas, 88
Erbe, Heather, 7
excellence, 6–7, 15, 21–29, 33, 55, 64, 68, 107, 109–11, 115–18

Flack, Judy, 8
Flood, Rev. Kelly, 57–58

Goodwin, Allen, 17
Grice, Jennifer, 13

Hampton, Tricia. *See* Cary, Tricia
Harmon, Rebecca, 117–18
Harrison, Sarah, 36
Hawkins, Ben, 41

Hawkins, Cynthia, 60
Henderson, Kimberly, 37–38
Herndon, Jina, 8, 16
Hughes, Patrick Henry, 1, 3, 37, 93, 107, 111–12. *See also* books: *I Am Potential* (by P. H. Hughes and P. J. Hughes)
Hughes, Patrick John, 2, 3, 107, 111–12. *See also* books: *I Am Potential* (by P. H. Hughes and P. J. Hughes)

Indiana University, 22

Jackson, Phil, 27
Jessie Clark Middle School, 60
Jones, Nola, 84

Kasarskis, Peter, 53–54
Keillor, Garrison, 22
Kennedy, Robert F., 21
Kentucky state marching band championships, 36–37
Ki-moon, Ban, 92
Kreisler, Fritz, 23

Lafayette High School, 1, 11, 60; marching band, 17, 23, 25, 28, 36–37, 44, 47–49, 53–54, 75, 84, 101–4, 117–18; symphonic band, 25, 35, 38, 40, 44, 47–49, 53–54, 59–60, 75
Lautzenheiser, Tim, 17, 28, 47, 55
leadership, 3, 7–8, 12, 43–54, 65–66, 110–11, 117–18
Lombardi, Vince, 18, 58

MacKenzie, David, 43
Macy's Thanksgiving Day Parade, 12
Magee, Terry, 49–50
Makris, Andreas, 77

Maslanka, David, 105, 107. *See also* music: Symphony No. 7 (by David Maslanka); *Testament* (by David Maslanka)
McGavock High School, 84
McMurray, Allan, 94
McNeal, Steve, 31
Middle Tennessee State University, 16–17
marching band, 40
Midwest International Band and Orchestra Clinic, 12–13, 23–25, 35, 52–53
Minor, Milton, 78, 117–18
Moore, J. Larry, 8, 16, 21, 24–25, 40, 43, 85–89, 99, 117–18
Moore, Jameson David, 105–6
Moore, Lorian Sena, 105–6
Muncey, Christy, 34
music: *Amazing Grace*, 79; *America, the Beautiful* (by Samuel Ward and Katharyn Lee Bates), 79, 94–95; *Chorale No. 12* (by J.S. Bach), 43; *CSU Alma Mater*, 77; *Danny Boy*, 101–4; *Devil Went Down to Georgia*, 100–101; *Georgia on My Mind*, 100–101; *Happy Birthday* (by Mildred H. Hill and Patty Smith Hill), 76–77; *Highlight from* Les Misérables, 49, 84; *La Forza del Destino* (by Giuseppe Verdi), 52; *Leader of the Band* (by Dan Fogelberg), 99; *Let It Be Me*, 100–101; *My Old Kentucky Home* (by Stephen Collins Foster), 1, 77–79; *O Magnum Mysterium* (by Lauridsen), 36, 111–13; *Ol' Man River*, 100–101; *Requiem* (by Johannes Brahms), 79; *Salvation Is Created* (by Tschesnokoff)), 100–101, 112–13; *The Star-Spangled Banner*, 79, 94; *Step to the Rear*, 75; *Sweet Georgia Brown*, 100–101; Symphony No. 7 (by David Maslanka), 105–6 (*see also* Maslanka, David); *Testament* (by David Maslanka), 106 (*see also* Maslanka, David); *We Shall Overcome*, 79

National Symphony Orchestra, 77
Nicholas, Chris, 57
New York Philharmonic, 79

Obama, Barack, 92
Ott, Jim, 100–101

Parks, George, 40
Pascal, Blaise, 99
Patrick, Patricia, 24
Paul Blazer High School, 24
performance wear, 72–75
Petraeus, Gen. David, 93
Picadome Elementary School, 48
Powell, Colin, 93

Rabin, Marvin, 39
Reagan, Ronald, 89
Redmond, Derek, 2
Reese, Carolyn, 8, 16, 22
Rehberg, L. Jerome, 40
Revelli, William, 26
Reynolds, Heather, 11–12
Reynolds, Madge, 11
Reynolds, Thurmas, 11, 36–37
Riley, Linda, 9
Roeder, Matthew, 94
Rumford, Kendra, 7
Rupp, Adolph, 18

Sames, Edward, 59–60
Schuller, Rev. Robert, 57, 82
Sena Moore, Kimberly, 7–8, 81,
    105–6
Smith, Robert W., 85
Spirit of Atlanta drum and bugle
    corps, 44, 63–64, 86, 100–101
Stamford, Bryant, 93
Stevens, Tyler, 48–49
Stone, Michael, 112–13

Thaut, Michael, 33
Toscanini, Arturo, 46
Transylvania University, 41
trombone "suicide routine," 68–69
tuning, 64–65, 67–68

U.S. Air Force, 53
U.S. Air Force Academy, 54
uniforms. *See* performance wear
University of Colorado, 93

University of Kentucky, 1, 13, 18, 32,
    39, 44, 50, 56
University of Louisville: marching
    band, 1–2, 78, 93, 107, 111–12
University of Massachusetts:
    marching band, 40
University of Michigan, 26
University of North Texas, 17
University of Pittsburgh, 117–18
University of South Carolina, 23, 58, 75

Virginia Commonwealth University, 50
Vizutti, Allen, 53

Walton, Sam, 76
Weekes, George "Pop," 8
Weekes, Sarah "Mom," 8
Wiencko, Christy. *See* Muncey,
    Christy
Williams, Mike, 117–18
Witherspoon, Elizabeth, 47

About the Author

J. Steven Moore is a career music educator who has developed nationally recognized programs of excellence at the secondary and collegiate level. He is chair of the Department of Music at the University of Central Missouri and has enjoyed serving as a music conductor at Colorado State University, the University of Kentucky, Central Kentucky Youth Orchestras, and Lafayette High School in Lexington, Kentucky.